Trauma-Sensitive Schools

Trauma-Sensitive Schools

The Importance of Instilling Grit, Determination, and Resilience

Colleen Lelli

ROWMAN & LITTLEFIELD
Lanham • Boulder • New York • London

Published by Rowman & Littlefield
An imprint of The Rowman & Littlefield Publishing Group, Inc.
4501 Forbes Boulevard, Suite 200, Lanham, Maryland 20706
www.rowman.com

6 Tinworth Street, London, SE11 5AL, United Kingdom

Copyright © 2021 by Colleen Lelli

All figures created by the author unless otherwise noted.

All rights reserved. No part of this book may be reproduced in any form or by any electronic or mechanical means, including information storage and retrieval systems, without written permission from the publisher, except by a reviewer who may quote passages in a review.

British Library Cataloguing in Publication Information Available

Library of Congress Cataloging-in-Publication Data

Names: Lelli, Colleen, 1973– author.
Title: Trauma-sensitive schools : the importance of instilling grit, determination, and resilience / Colleen Lelli.
Description: Lanham, Maryland : Rowman & Littlefield, 2021. | Includes bibliographical references. | Summary: "The purpose of this book is to both support schools in their creation of trauma sensitive school systems and classrooms and provide practical strategies for educators to implement in the classroom."—Provided by publisher.
Identifiers: LCCN 2020033369 (print) | LCCN 2020033370 (ebook) | ISBN 9781475849226 (cloth) | ISBN 9781475849233 (paperback) | ISBN 9781475849240 (epub)
Subjects: LCSH: Children with mental disabilities—Education. | School mental health services. | Psychic trauma in children. | School environment—Psychological aspects.
Classification: LCC LC4601 .L45 2021 (print) | LCC LC4601 (ebook) | DDC 371.92—dc23
LC record available at https://lccn.loc.gov/2020033369
LC ebook record available at https://lccn.loc.gov/2020033370

To my husband, Michael, my son, Michael, and my daughter, Julianna, for their willingness to love and support me (and keep up with the housework) while I finished this book. I would also like to thank my mom, dad, and sister Christine for their love and support. To my girlfriends (you know who you are)—without your words of wisdom, your ability to make me smile, and your encouragement, this would not have been possible. Lastly, to all of my students, past present, and future—my love of teaching is because of all of you, so I thank you all for the opportunity to live my dream job every day.

Contents

Preface ix

Acknowledgments xi

Introduction xiii

PART I: BACKGROUND KNOWLEDGE FOR CHILDREN OF TRAUMA   1

Chapter 1   What Does the Adverse Childhood Experiences Study Tell Us About Educating Children of Trauma?   3

PART II: HELP! IMPACT OF TRAUMA AND THE INTERVENTIONS TO SUCCESS   17

Chapter 2   A Domestic Violence Primer for Educators   19

Chapter 3   Impact of Trauma on Children Across Developmental Stages   35

Chapter 4   Impact of Trauma and the Interventions for Children's Language and Memory   49

Chapter 5   Impact of Trauma on Relationships and Self-Regulation   63

PART III: TOOLBOX WITH MORE STRATEGIES TO SUPPORT CHILDREN OF TRAUMA   81

Chapter 6   Supporting Reading and Writing Skills for Children of Trauma   83

Chapter 7	The Healing Power of Children's Literature	97
Chapter 8	Creating Trauma-Sensitive Schools: The Importance of Mental Health Awareness and Positive School Climate	111
Chapter 9	Teaching Resilience, Grit, and Determination	129
Chapter 10	Practicing Self-Care for Educators	145
About the Author		157

Preface

As a young educator with a brand-new classroom in the mid-1990s, I sometimes wondered if some of my students' home lives and past traumatic experiences affected their learning. I was a high school learning support and emotional support teacher, and many of my students were very disenchanted with learning and schooling in general. It was hard to get them to achieve or even recognize what they *could* achieve. What I have learned since then is the distinct difference between what Carol Dweck identifies as a growth mindset and a fixed mindset. My favorite part of the job were the connections I was able to make with the students: the relationships and watching them succeed—even when they exhibited a fixed mindset.

Now, as a college professor, I am still seeing students struggle and face challenges both inside and outside the classroom. Some have disclosed recent or past traumas and as a result displayed a fixed mindset. Others have left me wondering if they are suffering as a result of trauma. As a result of my dissertation and follow-up research, I decided to start exploring ways I could be better informed and implement trauma-informed practices within the college classroom.

I began to research trauma-informed practices with the seminal Adverse Childhood Experiences (ACE) Study from 1998. This study was a collaborative effort between the Centers for Disease Control and Prevention and Kaiser Permanente and was one of the largest studies published about adverse childhood experiences and their connections to health later in life. As a result of this study and the many others that have since followed, including research studies in the field of neuroscience, we now know the ways stress, chronic stress, and trauma can negatively impact a child's development.

Recent research from experts such as Ricky Greenwald and Dr. Bruce Perry recognizes that helping traumatized children does not have to take place in a clinical setting but can take place in nonclinical settings with people such as educators, caregivers, coaches, and family members. Daily supportive interactions from caring adults can bring healing while using strategies in a school setting that can promote learning for children of trauma.

We also know that chronic stress and trauma occur more frequently than we originally thought. We are better equipped to implement trauma-informed practices in the medical, judicial, and now the education field. As educators, regardless of the age we teach, whether it's preschool children or college students, we are recognizing the importance of supporting students affected by trauma. We are using a wide range of learning strategies, tools, and resources while creating safe, calm, and nurturing environments.

This book is an expansion of my doctoral work, research articles, and the many sessions I have provided at conferences, professional developments, and other speaking engagements over the past few years. The work contained here offers the strategies and tools necessary for implementing trauma-informed practices across school settings, classrooms, and before- and after-school programs. I have been very fortunate to work closely with an array of individuals including school administrators, educators, social workers, counselors, before- and after-school professionals, and college faculty and staff to raise awareness about the effects of adverse childhood experiences and provide them with the tools necessary to support students in the classroom.

When speaking with educators, we have shared the importance of implementing in the classroom, regardless of the age of the students, conversations and lessons on goal setting, to support and build resiliency. Furthermore, students can gain success and happiness by learning (and teaching) the components necessary to possess a growth mindset.

It is my hope that this book will provide you with the information necessary to assist your students affected by trauma and help to reduce the negative effects of stress and trauma. Educators and any adult working with children who is able to bond and make a connection with our young people need to know that they are heroes. It is because of those relationships that many children and young people are able to begin the healing process from their adverse childhood experiences.

Acknowledgments

I am indebted and so thankful for the many educators who supported me along the way as we walked on this journey together to bring this book to fruition. I would like to thank all of the teachers, administrators, before- and after-care professionals, coaches, and counselors who work with children every day and build the bonds that support them in their life's dreams. I would like to thank all of my family and friends for their support, especially my husband, Michael, and my kids, Michael and Julianna. Lastly, thank you to the reviewers of this text for their insight, expertise, and editing suggestions: Carolyn Berenato, Martha Waring Chaffee, Thomas Conway, Johanna Crocetto, Amber Gentile, Cathy Gibbons, Amy Persichetti, and Rina Vassallo.

Introduction

We see the same story and ensuing horror time and again. It could be any of the following: a school shooting; a suicide of a young person; physical, emotional, or sexual abuse of a child; or the terrible effects of bullying. The results have many asking why and those close to the victim(s) struggling to overcome their indescribable grief and sadness. The psychological damage is hard to overcome, and educators are on the front lines supporting these students.

Educators and those working in schools are undeniably in a position to support children who are struggling with traumatic experiences. The statistics are startling and over the past 10 years have not improved. About 45% of children under the age of 17 in the United States have experienced at least one adverse childhood experience, and 1 in 10 children nationally have experienced three or more Adverse Childhood Experiences (ACEs), placing them in a category where they are at especially high risk for mental, physical, and emotional health issues throughout their lifespan (National Survey of Children's Health [NSCH], 2016).

Educators need to ensure their classroom environment is a welcoming, compassionate, safe haven for all students who enter. Educators who understand the effects trauma can have on the mind, body, and especially the brain are better equipped to provide the supports necessary for them to succeed. School can be a place for healing and coping.

The purpose of this book is both to support schools in their creation of trauma-sensitive school systems and classrooms and to provide practical strategies for educators to implement in the classroom. The importance of understanding how trauma impacts cognitive, behavioral, and social growth is emphasized with key terms outlined and discussed. The information provided in this book can support educators, administrators, school staff, counselors, coaches, caregivers—anyone working with children and teens—in developing environments where children can not only survive but also thrive.

ORGANIZATION

This book is organized into three parts. Part I, "Background Knowledge for Children of Trauma," provides the reader with background knowledge regarding important concepts related to children of trauma. Chapter 1 is titled "What Does the Adverse Childhood Experiences Study Tell Us About Educating Children of Trauma?" This chapter explores and provides information about the seminal Adverse Childhood Experiences (ACE) Study. Neurobiological effects related to adverse childhood experiences are explored and the effects ACEs can have on educating those affected by trauma.

Part II, "Help! Impact of Trauma and the Interventions to Success," includes chapters 2, 3, 4, and 5 and explores the impact trauma can have on students and the various interventions that can be utilized to support young people affected by the detrimental effects of trauma.

Chapter 2, "A Domestic Violence Primer for Educators," is an expansion and continuation of my doctoral work focused on educating preservice teachers about the effects domestic violence can have on all victims, including the children in the household while the abuse is occurring.

Chapter 3 is titled "Impact of Trauma on Children Across Developmental Stages" and delivers various child developmental theories and then, subsequently, describes the ways trauma can affect child development at various stages in the developmental process.

In chapter 4, I explain the "Impact of Trauma and the Interventions for Children's Language and Memory." Specifically explored are expressive and receptive language and the impact trauma can have on language skills and brain functioning. Furthermore, the impact that trauma-related incidences can have on short-term, working memory and long-term memory is provided. Lastly, strategies to support language development and long- and short-term memory are also given.

In chapter 5 I delve into the topic of the "Impact of Trauma on Relationships and Self-Regulation." The three categories explaining infant and toddler attachment styles are introduced, and the ways that trauma can affect attachment is further detailed. Information about the stress-response system and using the system in a positive manner to self-regulate feelings and behaviors is specified. Teacher-student relationships are also explored, and strategies to support developing relationships and self-regulation are provided. Many times, attachment theory is explored in the field of social work and not in great detail in the field of education. This makes this chapter very unique to other books on the market about children affected by trauma.

Part III, "Toolbox with More Strategies to Support Children of Trauma" includes chapters 6–10 and offers further information about educating students and supporting their reading and writing acquisition. Using children's literature to support children of trauma, the significance of mental health awareness and the necessity for a positive school climate are investigated next. Lastly, the importance of practicing self-care as educators is identified, an area that is so often neglected.

In chapter 6, titled, "Supporting Reading and Writing Skills for Children of Trauma," I explore the effects trauma can have on expressive and receptive skills and the strategies to use in the classroom for children of trauma to successfully improve expressive and receptive language skills.

Chapter 7, "The Healing Power of Children's Literature," is also an expansion of my doctoral work. Here, I provide a brief history of the term *bibliotherapy* and the ways to implement this practice, as well as book lists to support the selection of quality trauma-related literature for various age groups.

Chapter 8, "Creating Trauma-Sensitive Schools: The Importance of Mental Health Awareness and Positive School Climate," signifies the importance of mental health awareness and a positive school climate. This chapter suggests best practices to build a positive school climate. I discuss Social Emotional Learning (SEL) practices and curriculum that can be incorporated as a school-wide approach and within classrooms. I also present the Universal Design for Learning (UDL) framework as a way to implement positive school climate and trauma-informed practices. Lastly, specific definitions and resources to understand the roles of a mandated reporter are explored.

Chapter 9 is titled "Teaching Resilience, Grit, and Determination," and definitions are given for *resilience*, *grit*, and *growth mindset* and the ways these terms are connected to trauma. Models and frameworks, as well as strategies, are provided for designing curriculum to teach resiliency, grit, and growth mindset.

Many times, educators forget to take care of themselves. This can be detrimental to the education field, leading to burnout and high teacher turnover rates. In chapter 10, "Practicing Self-Care for Educators," the terms *secondary traumatic stress*, *compassion fatigue*, and *vicarious trauma* are discussed. *Self-care* is defined, and finally tips for self-care are provided.

***

You've taken the first step by reading this book to support your students and build positive relationships with them. I am optimistic this book will provide you with the tools and strategies to confidently encourage our youngest victims of trauma and chronic stress.

REFERENCE

National Survey of Children's Health. (2016). *Fast facts: 2016 National Survey of Children's Health*. Data Resource Center, supported by Cooperative Agreement U59MC27866 from the U.S. Department of Health and Human Services, Health Resources and Services Administration (HRSA), Maternal and Child Health Bureau (MCHB). www.childhealthdata.org

Part I

BACKGROUND KNOWLEDGE FOR CHILDREN OF TRAUMA

1

What Does the Adverse Childhood Experiences Study Tell Us About Educating Children of Trauma?

This chapter will provide:
- an explanation of the Adverse Childhood Experiences (ACEs) Study;
- the neurobiological effects of adverse childhood experiences; and
- information about the different types of stress, including: positive, acute, tolerable, and toxic stress.

EXPLANATION OF THE ADVERSE CHILDHOOD EXPERIENCES STUDY

Most recently, a report by the nonprofit group Child Trends found that most states have not adopted a comprehensive set of policies to address student well-being (Keierleber, 2019). In the same report, it was noted that nearly half of America's students have traumatic or adverse childhood experiences. Even more now than ever, our children need serious help. Schools and educators are in a position to provide the support necessary to ensure all children have a positive well-being.

The Adverse Childhood Experiences (ACEs) Study has proven to be a significant epidemiologic study to explain how childhood abuse, neglect, and other traumatic experiences could have an effect on well-being in adulthood. The original study was conducted from 1995 to 1997 by Vincent Felitti, M.D., from Kaiser Permanente and Robert Anda, M.D. In San Diego County, California, over 17,000 people who were being given physical exams at the San Diego Health Appraisal Clinic were asked to complete a confidential survey regarding their childhood experiences (up to age 18) and their current health status and behaviors. The survey results and the results of their physical exams were combined to form the study's findings.

The CDC-Kaiser ACEs study questions were developed from a number of published surveys such as the Conflicts Tactics Scales (Straus & Hamby, 2003), the 1988 National Health Interview Survey (as cited in Felitti et al., 1998), the Behavioral Risk Factor Surveys (as cited in Felitti et al., 1998), the Third National Health and Nutrition Examination Survey (as cited in Felitti et al., 1998), and lastly the Diagnostic Interview Schedule of the National Institute of Mental Health (NIMH) (as cited in Felitti et al., 1998).

From these surveys, 17 questions were developed and organized for the ACEs study. There were a total of 10 types of childhood trauma measured in the ACEs study. The ACEs study was broken down into three major categories: abuse, neglect, and household dysfunction. Five of these traumas consisted of abuse and neglect categories that occurred to the person completing the questionnaire. Abuse was comprised of physical, emotional, and sexual abuse. Neglect included physical and emotional.

The last five types of adversities related to other family members. These household dysfunctions included experiences such as having an incarcerated relative, having a family member diagnosed with mental illness or depression, having a family member with substance addictions or alcohol addictions, witnessing domestic abuse of a mother, and losing a parent to divorce, separation, or other reasons. The infographic in figure 1.1 depicts all the traumas that were measured in the ACEs study as well as the prevalence of ACEs and the possible risk outcomes as a result of these experiences.

There are many other types of childhood trauma—witnessing a sibling being abused, community violence, homelessness, food insecurity, being the victim of racism, or being bullied by a classmate—but only these 10 types, identified above, were measured because these were mentioned as the most common by a group of about 300 Kaiser members. They provide a useful marker for the severity of trauma experienced. Other types of trauma may have a similar impact.

Participants of the study were provided an ACE score. An ACE score is a total count of the number of adversities experienced in childhood from the above listed 10 categories. Each adversity counts as one, no matter how many times it occurs. The total score indicates the amount of stress during childhood, and as that number increases, so does the risk for other related health problems in adulthood.

Through this seminal research study, it was discovered that people with an ACE score of more than 4 were at risk of cancer and heart disease, 5 or more ACEs signified that an individual was 8 times at risk of becoming an alcoholic. Finally, people with an ACE score of 6 or higher were at risk of their

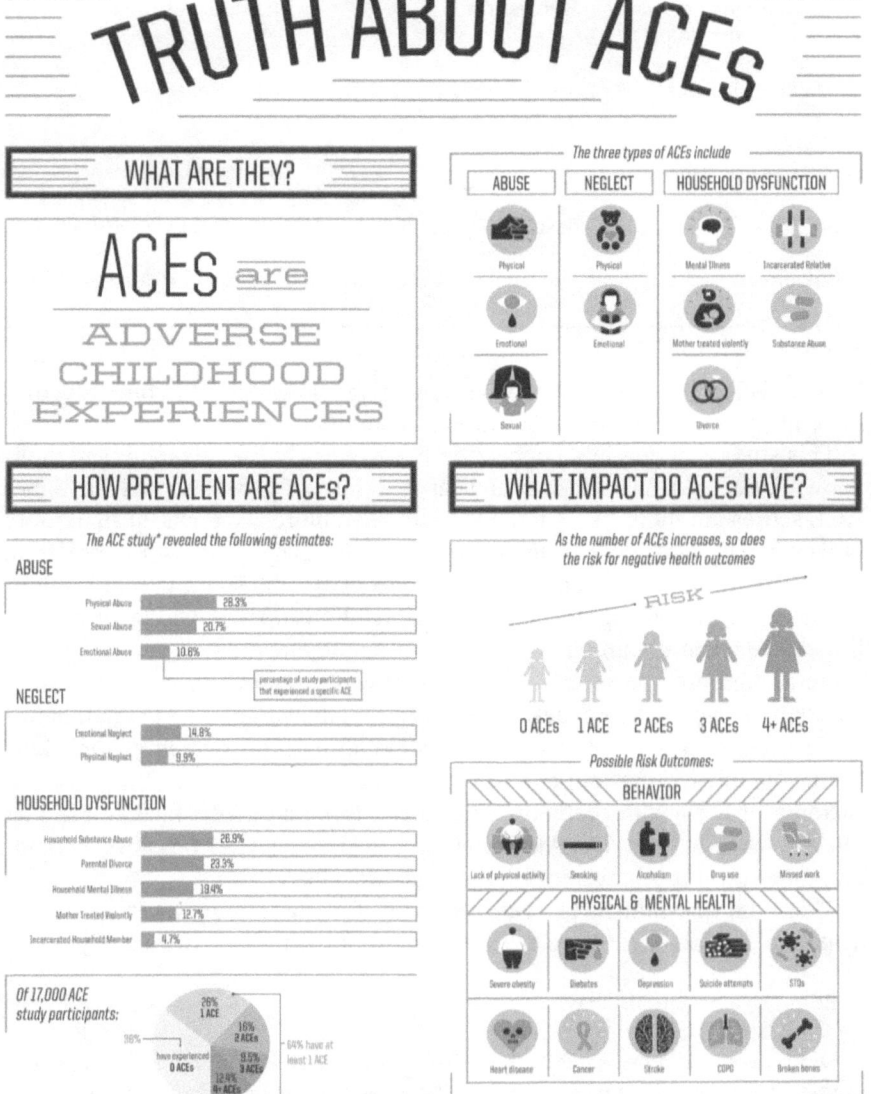

Figure 1.1 Adverse Childhood Experiences or ACEs. *Source:* Copyright 2013, Robert Wood Johnson Foundation. Used with permission from the Robert Wood Johnson Foundation.

Table 1.1. Health Difficulties and Risk Factors as a Result of Adverse Childhood Experiences

Alcoholism and alcohol abuse	Stomach ulcers	Suicide attempts
Early initiation of sexual activity and multiple sexual partners	Depression	Illicit drug use
Chronic Obstructive Pulmonary Disease (COPD)	Risk for intimate partner violence	Liver disease
Greater risk of asthma	Fetal death	Unintended pregnancies and adolescent pregnancies
Migraines	Sexually Transmitted Diseases (STDs)	Ischemic Heart Disease (IHD)
Reflux disease	Smoking and early initiation of smoking	Autoimmune diseases

Source: Felitti (1998)

lifespan being shortened by 20 years, and given an exposure to one category, there is an 80% likelihood of exposure to another.

This study resulted in a connection between early life adversity and well-known killers like heart disease and cancer (Harris, 2018). People with higher ACE scores are more likely to be violent, have more accidents, sustain more broken bones, use more drug prescriptions, be diagnosed with depression, and suffer from autoimmune diseases (Anda et al., 2005). Further difficulties could result in creating and maintaining relationships, engaging in healthy life choices, and obtaining and sustaining employment (www.acestudy.org). More importantly, because of this study, it was not necessarily the intensity, duration, or negativity of these events, but it is the variety and the number of adverse experiences that is linked to potential harmful outcomes for adults (Peterson, 2014; Blaustein & Kinniburgh, 2010).

Some of the health problems and risk factors that adults face at a higher rate are listed in table 1.1. Also refer back to figure 1.1 for possible risk outcomes as a result of adverse childhood experiences.

There are questionnaires available today for use to assess and determine someone's ACE score. Here are a few questions from the ACEs study.

Prior to your 18th birthday:

Did a parent or other adult in the household often or very often . . . Swear at you, insult you, put you down, or humiliate you? or Act in a way that made you afraid that you might be physically hurt?
    No___ If Yes, enter 1 ___

Did you often or very often feel that . . . You didn't have enough to eat, had to wear dirty clothes, and had no one to protect you? or Your parents were too drunk or high to take care of you or take you to the doctor if you needed it?
No___ If Yes, enter 1 ___

Were your parents ever separated or divorced?
No___ If Yes, enter 1 ___

It's important to note that the ACE score is meant as a guide. As mentioned earlier in this chapter, other types of toxic stress or trauma could also place a person at risk for health, cognitive, and emotional consequences. ACE questions can be found here: https://acestoohigh.com/got-your-ace-score.

ACE Pyramid

The conceptual framework for the study and the mechanism by which adverse childhood experiences can affect health and well-being throughout the life span is best demonstrated through the ACE pyramid (see figure 1.2).

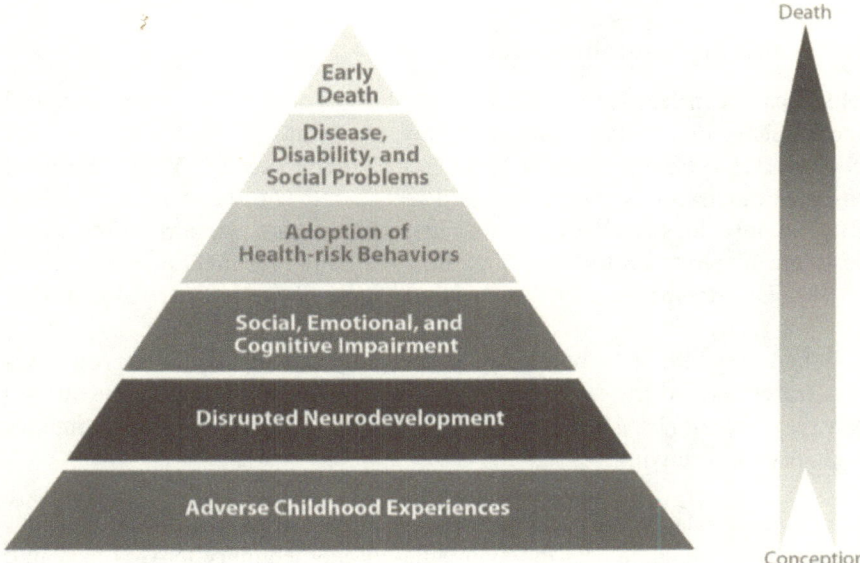

Mechanism by Which Adverse Childhood Experiences Influence Health and Well-being Throughout the Lifespan

Figure 1.2   Adverse Childhood Experiences and health and well-being throughout the lifespan. *Source:* Center for Disease Control (CDC). Retrieved from https://www.cdc.gov/violenceprevention/acestudy/ACE_graphics.html

Dr. Robert Anda believes that the pyramid serves as a life course model. He further asserts from the research completed since the beginning study in the 1990s that more is now known about how biology can affect the lifespan beginning with preconception. Neuroscience research has proven there are biological impairments—including cognitive disconnect—that may be present as a result of ACEs.

As this model serves as a prevention model, some of the guiding questions utilizing this model include: (1) What are the risk factors for disease, disability, and social problems that lead to early death; and (2) Can we modify them to reduce the risks that move through the lifespan? Many of these risks formulate what Dr. Anda (2005) identifies as risk clusters, which could include health risks such as management of diabetes, hypertension, smoking, treating mental illnesses, and so on (see table 1.1 and figure 1.1 above).

Dr. Anda and his colleagues (2005) were interested in finding if there are experiences that lead to these risk clusters. Primary prevention would be a way to thwart or understand these risk clusters. This was the underlying hypotheses or questions and the result of the formation of the Adverse Childhood Experiences (Center for Advanced Studies in Child Welfare, 2014).

ACEs and the Neurobiological Effects

Much has been learned since the original ACE study. The neurobiological mechanisms of childhood adversity are becoming better understood. Dr. Nadine Burke Harris, founder and CEO of the Center for Youth Wellness in San Francisco's Bayview Hunter Point, along with her team discovered that not only does the body sense danger and set off a firestorm of chemical reactions aimed to protect itself, but also the body *remembers* (Harris, 2018, p. 48). The stress-response system is our *fight*, *flight*, or *freeze* system (see textbox 1.1).

When responding to acute stress, the body's sympathetic nervous system (often termed the "fight or flight response") is activated by the sudden release of hormones. The "team" involved in this sudden release of hormones includes the following:

- The amygdala is the brain's fear center, located next to the Hippocampus. The amygdala sets the sympatho-adrenomedullary (SAM) axis into motion. SAM is the system that speeds up the heart, and without conscious thought allows us to respond to danger situations.
- The hippocampus processes emotional information and is critical for long-term memories and spatial navigation.

> **Textbox 1.1**
> What does fight, flight, or freeze look like in children? Many times, trauma or toxic stress can cause the brain to adapt to survive—otherwise known as fight, flight, or freeze. Once the brain has been triggered, these behaviors can be exhibited in various ways and educators will notice these behaviors in the classroom. Basically, the part of the brain responsible for "feeling" is overcome by the "thinking" brain. Internalizing or externalizing behaviors may be exhibited as the normal developmental process is interrupted. The following are a few ways these externalizing and internalizing behaviors are connected to the fight, flight, and freeze system.
>
> - Fight: We will see children with physically aggressive behaviors. Teachers may consider these children to be "hyperactive" or display "oppositional behaviors."
> - Flight: Internalizing behaviors are exhibited, such as avoidance, escaping, withdrawal, or isolation.
> - Freeze: Children may look dazed, daydream, shut down, emotionally or exhibit forgetfulness.

- The prefrontal cortex is the front part of the brain that regulates executive functioning—in other words, it acts like a conductor and helps to coordinate the various parts of the brain. Both the hippocampus and the prefrontal cortex interact to support working memory and long-term memory.

Unlike the SAM axis, the hypothalamic-pituitary adrenal (HPA) axis continues to be activated long after the stressor has been removed. The HPA axis controls levels of cortisol by the adrenal glands. This axis is thought of as the body's energy regulator since it is responsible for regulating many of the hormones. Increased cortisol is released from the adrenal cortex when a person is under a stressful situation for more than a few minutes. The paraventricular nucleus (PVN) in the hypothalamus controls the release of the cortisol and corticotrophin-releasing hormone (CRH) in response to stress. CRH then acts on the pituitary gland, which releases adrenocorticotrophic hormone (ACTH). Cortisol is then released from the adrenal cortex. See figures 1.3 and 1.4 depicting the stress response system and the HPA axis.

So, all that being said, what happens to a child's brain and body when they are continuously experiencing adverse situations? Is the stress response system, specifically the HPA, impacted when children are faced repeatedly with adverse experiences?

Jacqueline Bruce and her colleagues (2009) set out to explore these questions. They analyzed cortisol levels of 117 foster kids and 60 low-income kids

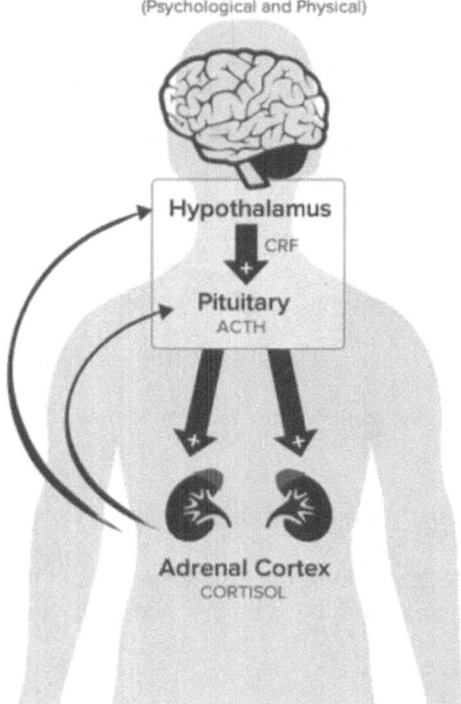

Figure 1.3 Stress response system. *Source:* Integrative Therapeutics Image. Retrieved from https://www.integrativepro.com/Resources/Integrative-Blog/2016/The-HPA-Axis

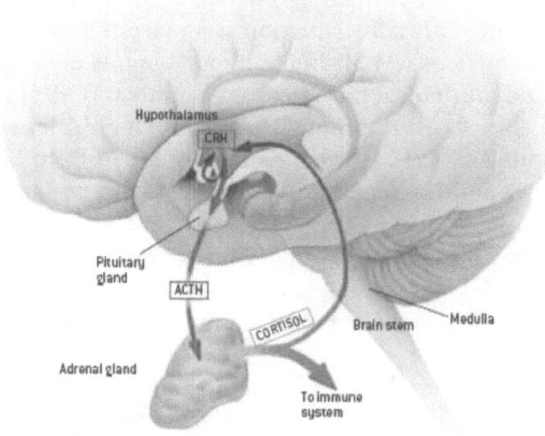

Figure 1.4 HPA axis and the stress response system. *Source:* Roberto Osti. Retrieved from https://classconnection.s3.amazonaws.com/1527/flashcards/749837/png/hpa-axis-and-stress-response.png

who were not maltreated to determine if adverse experiences had an effect on the functioning of the stress-response system and the HPA axis. They found that the foster kids showed dysregulated cortisol levels in comparison to the kids who had not experienced the same adverse experiences.

One interesting piece from this study were the similarities, and yet extreme differences, between the control group and the experimental group. Demographically, both groups lived in the same area. The low-income kids or the control group were all living with one parent but had not had contact with child services, which means that they were not maltreated. The control group had been exposed to some level of adversity, *but* their cortisol levels were not abnormal. Many face adversity, and children can experience stress without a dysregulated stress response system.

Basically, when the stress response system is activated too frequently or if the stressor is too intense, the body can lose the ability to shut down the HPA and SAM axes (Harris, 2018, p. 53). Dr. Nadine Burke Harris (2018) explains this system as the body's stress thermostat, and it is broken when this phenomenon occurs, otherwise known as the disruption of feedback inhibition. The body just keeps blasting cortisol through their system, and this is exactly what Bruce and associates (2009) were finding.

THREE DIFFERENT KINDS OF STRESS

There are varying degrees of stress that can affect a body. Some of this stress, known as positive stress, is actually needed and helpful to build persistence, grit, and determination. Positive stress is normal stress and part of healthy development. The heart rate increases for a brief period of time, and hormone levels are somewhat elevated. This "jolt" will focus a child's attention and therefore is considered healthy. An example of a positive stress moment would be receiving an immunization, a visit to the dentist, or a child starting a new school. Many athletes may experience pregame jitters, and those feelings would be another example of positive stress.

Acute and tolerable stress may actually increase memory performance, while excessive levels and chronic stress may have negative effects in memory functioning. Tolerable stress is a more severe reaction that activates the body's alert systems to a greater degree as a result of more severe, longer-lasting difficulties. Some examples of these include loss or serious illness of a loved one or a parent's divorce (National Scientific Council on the Developing Child [NSCDC], 2005).

When stress becomes more intense, it can turn into toxic stress or even trauma.

Toxic stress is characterized by severe, frequent, and/or ongoing and prolonged activation of the stress response system (NSCDC, 2005). Such experiences could include: physical or emotional abuse, neglect, caregiver substance abuse or mental illness, exposure to violence, and/or economic hardship. Again, toxic stress is associated with important changes in the structure of neural, endocrine, and immune systems. Secondary changes also occur in behavior and metabolism.

A growing body of neuroscience research suggests that experiencing trauma during a critical developmental period, such as childhood, can lead to toxic stress that "disrupts brain architecture, affects other organ systems, and leads to stress-management systems that establish relatively lower thresholds for responsiveness that persist throughout life, thereby increasing the risk of stress-related disease and cognitive impairment well into the adult years" (Shonkoff et al., 2009, p. 256). Figure 1.5 depicts the following levels of stress: positive stress, tolerable stress, and toxic stress.

Early in a child's development, exposure to toxic stress can enact a long-term negative effect because of the brain's vulnerability at this time. During these early stages of development, cognitive and emotional preparation for a successful life is determined. If there is prolonged activation of the stress response system without a nurturing caregiver, long-term changes in the brain's structure will occur. This process is called "biological embedding" of an experience (Shonkoff, 2012). Adequate adult support can help a child negotiate the constant stress, but without that support, the child will suffer immeasurable damage, regardless of the child's age.

If toxic stress is occurring early in childhood, memory problems and the ability for an individual to learn can be negatively impacted. Later in childhood and adolescence, many areas of the brain are developed, and exposure to toxic stress during this period can result in difficulty in paying attention as well as impulse and emotional control. Consequences for exposure to toxic stress in late adolescence and early adulthood show heightened fear response and hyperactivity (Shonkoff, 2012).

The extended use of the fight-or-flight system can lead to the disruption of brain development and damage of various organ systems, which could impact physiological, psychological, and behavioral impairments over one's lifespan. Toxic stress can lead to cognitive impairment, learning disorders, heart disease, strokes, diabetes, immune dysfunction, depression, anxiety

| Mild or Positive Stress | Tolerable or Moderate Stress | Toxic or Chronic Stress | Trauma |

Figure 1.5 Leveling of stress. *Source:* Colleen Lelli

disorders, bipolar disorder, substance abuse, and an inability to regulate mood, behavior, and emotions (NSCDC, 2005).

Exposure to toxic stress has significant effects on all aspects of life. Because all of these impacts can have an insurmountable effect on learning, it is extremely important that educators intervene in ways to address positive strategies for the classroom.

ACES AND EFFECTS ON EDUCATION

We now know from the plethora of research that trauma is prevalent in the lives of children. We know that trauma affects learning and school performance as well as causing grave physical and emotional anguish. The following statistics have proven these facts:

- Data suggest that every classroom has at least one student affected by trauma.
- 68% of children and adolescents experienced at least one potential traumatic event by age 16. (Copeland et al., 2007; Cook et al., 2005).

Now that we understand the biology of trauma and the effects trauma and toxic stress can have on a child, the question then becomes: How can we best help them in an education setting? Schools have an important role to play in meeting the social and emotional needs of students. With the support of state departments of education, trauma-sensitive school systems can be developed to help children feel safe and provide the best environment for children to learn.

We will need to use strategies that will best encourage children of trauma. We need to understand their dysregulated stress systems. We need to change school culture and climate, but in doing so we *also* need to teach other important skills like grit, determination, and resilience. We need classroom strategies to support students learning reading, writing, and math skills. Lastly, we need to consider the ways teachers are affected by teaching and treating children of trauma and the effects this can have on their emotional well-being. Educators need to be further trained in self-care strategies.

In future chapters, the tools and strategies to support all learners in the K–12 classroom will be delivered. Empowering change by building grit, determination, and resilience will lead to mastery of skills, which will encourage children of trauma to lead productive and healthy lives.

REFERENCES

Anda, R. F., Felitti, V. J., Bremner, J. D., Walker, J. D., Whitfield, C., Perry, B. D., Dube, S. R., & Giles, W. H. (2006, April). The enduring effects of abuse and related adverse experiences in childhood. A convergence of evidence from neurobiology and epidemiology. *European Archives of Psychiatry and Clinical Neuroscience, 256*(3), 174–186. doi:10.1007/s00406-005-0624-4

Blaustein, M., & Kinniburgh, K. (2010). *Treating traumatic stress in children and adolescents.* Guilford Press.

Bruce, J., Fisher, P. A., Pears, K. C., & Levine, S. (2009). Morning cortisol levels in preschool-aged foster children: Differential effects of maltreatment type. *Developmental Psychobiology, 51*(1), 14–23.

Center for Advanced Studies in Child Welfare. (2014, August 26). *Impact of Adverse Childhood Experiences on health across the life course—core story: The ACE study.* https://www.youtube.com/watch?v=F4fBdHHsj5A

Cook, A., Spinazzola, J., Ford, J., Lanktree, C., Blaustein, M., Clotire, M., DeRosa, R., Hubbard, R., Kagan, R., Liautaud, J., Mallah, K., Olafson, E., & van der Kolk, B. (2005). Complex trauma in children and adolescents. *Psychiatry Annals, 35*(5), 390–398.

Copeland, W. E., Keeler, G., Angold, A., & Costello, E. J. (2007). Traumatic events and posttraumatic stress in childhood. *Arch Gen Psychiatry, 64*(5), 577–584. doi:10.1001/archpsyc.64.5.577. https://jamanetwork.com/journals/jamapsychiatry/fullarticle/482289

Felitti, V. J. (1998). Relationship of childhood abuse and household dysfunction to many of the leading causes of death in adults. *American Journal of Preventive Medicine, 14*(4), 245–258.

Harris, N. B. (2018). *The deepest well: Healing the long-term effects of childhood adversity.* Houghton Mifflin Harcourt.

Keierleber, M. (2019, January 31). *Despite prevalent trauma, from school shootings to the opioid epidemic, few states have policies to fully address student needs, study finds.* https://www.the74million.org/despite-prevalent-trauma-from-school-shootings-to-the-opioid-epidemic-few-states-have-policies-to-fully-address-student-needs-study-finds/?fbclid=IwAR3XteJOrTSvDTvzTDa3HbvEV9ybAd3lb7YTcBK0BsMn8yZNdn2AHOZQhcU

National Scientific Council on the Developing Child. (2005). *Excessive stress disrupts the architecture of the developing brain: Working paper #3.* http://developingchild.harvard.edu/index.php/resources/reports_and_working_papers/working_papers/wp3

Peterson, K. L. (2014). *Helping them heal: How teachers can support young children who experience stress and trauma.* Gryphon House.

Shonkoff, J. P. (2012). Leveraging the biology of adversity to address the roots of disparities in health and development. *Proceedings of the National Academy of Sciences.* http://www.pnas.org/cgi/doi/10.1073/pnas1121259109

Shonkoff, J. P., Boyce, W. T., & McEwen, B. S. (2009). Neuroscience, molecular biology, and the childhood roots of health disparities: Building a new framework for health promotion and disease prevention. *JAMA, 301*, 2252–2259.

Straus, M. A., & Hamby, S. L. (2003). *Conflict Tactics Scales*. WPS Publishing.

Part II

HELP! IMPACT OF TRAUMA AND THE INTERVENTIONS TO SUCCESS

2

A Domestic Violence Primer for Educators

This chapter will provide:

- definitions related to domestic violence and intimate partner violence (IPV);
- theoretical perspectives and models that examine domestic violence; and
- an examination of domestic violence as a human rights issue.

The study by Finkelhor and colleagues (2014) indicates that 17.9% of children of all ages have been exposed to physical intimate partner violence in their lifetime, or about 13.6 million children. The effects of this violence are widespread and endemic, but because children are resilient, age-appropriate education and intervention can mitigate complications in the emotional and cognitive growth in children.

Physical violence against women, and to a lesser extent against men, is a public health problem that has reached epidemic proportions (Breiding et al., 2015; Exner-Cortens et al., 2017). Domestic violence, also known as partner abuse, spouse-abuse, battering, or intimate partner violence (IPV), is one facet of the larger problem of family violence that affects millions of Americans and occurs across the lifespan (Breiding et al., 2015). Family violence includes persons within a family and encompasses the areas of child abuse and elder abuse as well as domestic violence.

Domestic violence distinguishes itself from other forms of family violence such as child abuse and elder abuse because the abuse occurs between intimate partners such as husbands and wives, in same sex marriages, or in other romantic partnerships. Not surprisingly, domestic violence, child abuse, and neglect frequently occur together (Edleson, 1999a; 1999b); however, the nature and dynamic of IPV differ from other forms of family violence in ways that are significant enough to warrant an independent discussion of this dynamic.

Because of the frequency of domestic violence and the impact it has on children who witness this violence in their homes, it is essential for teachers, counselors, social workers, and other child advocates to have sufficient knowledge about signs of domestic violence to appropriately educate and help these students. Therefore, teachers should be trained to recognize the signs or symptoms of domestic violence.

DEFINING *DOMESTIC VIOLENCE*

Intimate partner violence or *domestic violence* describes physical violence, sexual violence, stalking, and psychological aggression (including coercive acts) by a current or former intimate partner (Breiding et al., 2015). Despite many myths to the contrary, intimate partner violence knows no boundaries and occurs at all levels of socioeconomic status, and in every, ethnicity, culture, and religion. However, Buckley and colleagues (2007) identify several risk factors that increase the likelihood of domestic violence, including poverty, child abuse, parental substance abuse, unemployment, homelessness, and involvement in crime.

In the United States, one in four women has experienced severe abuse from an intimate partner (Black et al., 2011), and one in seven men has been a victim of severe physical violence by an intimate partner in their lifetime (Breiding et al., 2015). If sexual violence and stalking perpetrated by an intimate partner during a person's lifetime were also to be factored in, then the statistics are a bit higher—more than one in three women in the United States (37%) and more than one in four men (31%) are affected (Smith et al., 2017). The majority of incarcerated men today witnessed or experienced violence as children in their own homes (Sun et al., 2017).

IPV occurs on a continuum and can vary in frequency and severity. Episodes may have lasting impact and could have severe episodes over a period of years. Many times, children witness domestic violence or are relied on to provide support, protection, and consolation in the aftermath of a violent episode. In fact, approximately 40% to 50% of children have reported witnessing abuse (Holden, 2003).

Physical and sexual assaults—or threats to commit them—are the most prevalent types of violence that occur in relationships; however, there are other behaviors that abusers display that make up a larger system of abuse. Other behaviors or terms associated with domestic violence are defined in sidebar 2.1. Cyclical abuse, interspersed with periods of relative calm, allows

Sidebar 2.1. Intimate Partner Violence Definitions

1. Physical violence: Deliberate use of physical force to cause possible harm, injury, or even death. The following is considered physical violence; however, this is list is not exhaustive: scratching; shoving; throwing; grabbing; biting; choking; shaking; hair pulling; slapping; punching; hitting; burning; use of a weapon; and use of restraints. Coercing others to commit these acts is also considered an act of physical violence.
2. Sexual violence: The following five categories of sexual violence occur without the victim's free consent, including if the victim is unable to give consent due to intoxication or through voluntary or involuntary drug or alcohol use.
    - Rape or penetration of victim—Penetration is forced and occurs through the use of physical force against the victim or threat of physical force. These acts are unwanted vaginal, oral, or anal insertion and can be completed or attempted.
    - Victim was made to penetrate someone else—Victim could be made to sexually penetrate a perpetrator or someone else without the victim's consent.
    - Nonphysically pressured unwanted penetration—Victim was forced verbally or with the use of intimidation to consent or comply to being penetrated.
    - Unwanted sexual contact—The perpetrator will make the victim touch him/her either directly or through their clothing without the victim's consent.
    - Noncontact unwanted sexual experiences—Unwanted sexual occurrences that are not physical in nature and occur without the victim's consent. Taking or disseminating photographs of a sexual nature, threats of sexual violence, unwanted exposure to sexual situations like pornography, and verbal or behavioral sexual harassment are all examples of unwanted sexual experiences.
3. Stalking: Fear for one's own safety or the safety of a loved one is caused when there is a pattern of frequent (two or more occasions), unwanted contact. A few examples could include: phone calls, texts, emails, leaving of cards, letters, or other items not wanted by the victim; observing or following from a distance; damaging the victim's property or causing harm or threatening to cause injury to the victim's pet; and making physical threats to injure the victim or the victim's loved ones.
4. Psychological aggression can include verbal or nonverbal communication with the intent to cause harm or exert control over another person.

(continued)

> **Sidebar 2.1. continued**
>
> Aggression could cause mental or emotional despair. According to the Center for Disease Control (2017),
>
> > psychological aggression can include expressive aggression (e.g., name-calling, humiliating); coercive control (e.g., limiting access to transportation, money, friends, and family; excessive monitoring of whereabouts); threats of physical or sexual violence; control of reproductive or sexual health (e.g., refusal to use birth control; coerced pregnancy termination); exploitation of victim's vulnerability (e.g., immigration status, disability); exploitation of perpetrator's vulnerability; and presenting false information to the victim with the intent of making them doubt their own memory or perception (e.g., mind games).
>
> *Source:* Center for Disease Control (2017).

the abuser to gain power and control over the victim's life. As a result, domestic violence can negatively impact parenting styles.

Teachers may witness unhealthy parental dynamics during school events where parents are present, like parent-teacher conferences. A teacher may witness a parent who is a victim acting in an excessively controlling or authoritarian manner. On the other hand, a parent may be overly permissive or afraid to discipline the child (Phifer & McPherson, 2013). Depression or other mental difficulties may surface as a result of the continuous stress or psychological trauma, which could lead to difficulty in implementing positive parenting techniques (Cunningham & Baker, 2007).

DOMESTIC VIOLENCE AWARENESS THEORIES OR MODELS

Experts in partner violence describe three dominant models of couple dynamics: a cycle of abuse, Family Systems Theory, and the Duluth Model, popularly known as the Power and Control Wheel (Burge et al., 2015). Each model explains how dominance over a victim is attained and sustained.

In 1979, Lenore Walker (as explained in Burge et al., 2015) developed the cycle of abuse as a way to explain patterns of behavior in relationships. To an outside observer, it may seem counterintuitive for a victim to remain with an abuser. However, it is important to note that abusive relationships are not always in a state of crisis. Instead, abusive relationships follow a distinctive pattern.

During the first phase of abuse, considered the tension-building phase, verbal or minor physical abuse may transpire, and the abuser will alter their behavior to avoid conflict. Tension continues to build, which leads to an explosion. Phase 2 is a physical altercation that will be brief and brutal as the abuser demonstrates a total lack of control.

Afterward, phase 3 is the reconciliation or honeymoon phase, in which the abuser is filled with remorse, guilt, and/or fear that the victim will leave or call the police. The abuser will apologize and shower with gifts, love, and affection. Often, the abuser will make promises that it will never happen again.

Finally, in phase 4, there is calm and peace. The abuser may agree to counseling, ask for forgiveness, and create a normal atmosphere. In this model, sometimes phase 3 and 4 are combined, or phase 4 is often considered a component of the honeymoon or reconciliation phase.

Family Systems Theory is used to explain different aspects of abuse and family violence by exploring relationships within the family and the interconnectedness of the members (MacKay, 2012). Family Systems Theory is based on assumptions about relationship processes within families (Murray, 2006).

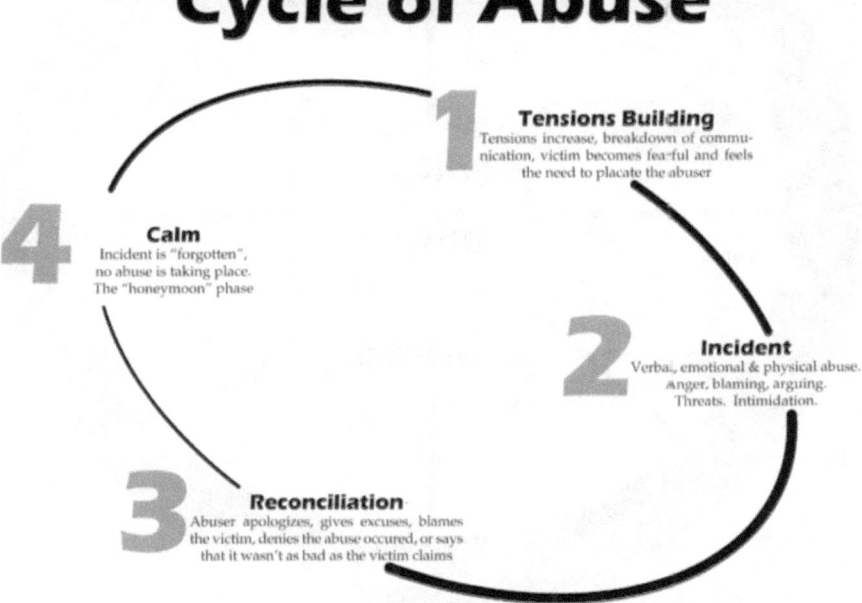

Figure 2.1 A depiction of the cycle of abuse. *Source:* Avanduyn [Public domain]. Retrieved from https://commons.wikimedia.org/wiki/File:Cycle_of_Abuse.png

Circular causality, a construct within this theory, maintains that events, within family dynamics are a result of multiple causes. Other theoretical assumptions point to the importance of intergenerational family processes, the significance of all forms of communication within families, and the regulation of family systems through explicit and implicit rules, information, and feedback (Murray, 2006). Family Systems Theory actively avoids labeling behaviors as good or bad. Instead, Family Systems Theory examines the function of the behavior within the context of the family.

Because Family Systems Theory fails to address the power of dynamics in families, there are many vocal critics of this approach (Babcock & La Taillade, 2000; Saunders, 2001). Some critics have argued that a failure to address power dynamics contributes to an assumption that each individual within a violent family system shares equal responsibility and power. Another critique holds that Family Systems Theory and the treatment of perpetrators

Figure 2.2 Power and control wheel. *Source:* Domestic Abuse Intervention Programs, The Duluth Model. Retrieved from www.duluthmodel.org

of family violence contribute to further excuses for the violent behavior and may provide the perpetrator with additional information to use to manipulate the victim (Saunders, 2001). Although these challenges and critiques exist for Family Systems Theory, many in the field remain focused on improving prevention and treatment strategies for families whose lives have been touched by violence (Murray, 2006).

The third theory, the Duluth Model, uses the Power and Control Wheel to describe violence as a series of behaviors used to control a partner's actions. The Duluth Model was created by the Domestic Abuse Intervention Programs (DAIP) (Bohall et al., 2016). It is the most commonly used intervention in the United States and Canada for men who are convicted of a domestic assault offense and mandated by the courts to receive treatment. The creators of this model assert that abuse is a constant force in victims' lives.

Unlike the cycle of violence theory, where abusive behaviors are interspersed with periods of calm, the Duluth Model maintains that the abuser uses controlling behaviors as part of a continuous pressure to subjugate the victim. While the physical violence may be sporadic, the controlling tactics are constant. This conceptual framework illustrates the complexity of domestic abuse. Researchers found eight nonphysical abusive behaviors exhibited by abusive men: coercion, denying, emotional abuse, intimidation, isolation, using children, male privilege, and economic control (Pence & Paymar, 1993).

Preconceptions exist regarding domestic violence. Many do not understand the intricacies in the power and control involved in these relationships. Many of these misconceptions are related to what we have been told or have been perpetuated by society in general. Sidebar 2.2 outlines the myths and realities regarding domestic violence.

Sidebar 2.2. Myths and Realities of Domestic Violence

Myth 1: Domestic violence only occurs in low-income families, ethnic minority families, uneducated families, or lower-socioeconomic-status families.
Reality: Abuse permeates every ethnic and social setting. The internal need for power, which drives abuse, does not relate to social standing, income, or ethnicity. Almost half (47.5%) of American Indian/Alaska Native women, 45.1% of non-Hispanic Black women, 37.3% of non-Hispanic White women, 34.4% of Hispanic women, and 18.3% of Asian-Pacific Islander women experience contact sexual violence, physical violence, and/or stalking by an intimate partner in their lifetime (CDC, 2017).

(continued)

Sidebar 2.2. continued

Myth 2: Domestic violence is an anger-control issue.
Reality: Domestic violence has nothing to do with anger. Anger is one of many tools an abuser uses to solicit power and control. One of the many reasons we know that abusers are in control of their anger is the fact that they often direct physical abuse on the body where the bruises are less likely to show. Furthermore, the abuser will wait until there are no witnesses to physically assault the victim.

Myth 3: Stalking is not a signal of a domestic violence relationship.
Reality: Stalking is part of the controlling behavior exhibited in a domestic violence relationship. In fact, nearly 90% of domestic violence homicide victims were both stalked and beaten in the year prior to their deaths (cited in Snyder, 2019). Furthermore, Snyder (2019) states that stalking is a crime in all 50 states.

Myth 4: Any woman who stays with her abuser is mentally weak.
Reality: Women have many reasons for staying in abusive relationships. Some women may not have access to money; they may stay because they have children and don't want to be in a broken marriage; the abused person may be isolated from their family and friends because the abuser has controlled the relationship, and some women feel they don't deserve better. Religious reasons and social stigma also deter women from leaving. There are other staggering and scary facts: (1) When domestic violence victims attempt to leave the relationship, the stalking and violence almost always escalate sharply as the perpetrator attempts to regain control. (2) The majority of domestic violence homicides occur as a woman attempts to leave or after she has left. (3) The most serious domestic violence injuries are perpetrated against women who have separated from the perpetrator.

Myth 5: Children aren't aware and are not affected by the violence in their homes.
Reality: Children are considered the hidden victims of domestic violence or IPV. Children suffer emotional, cognitive, behavioral, and developmental impairments as a result of witnessing domestic violence in the home. However, children are resilient, and once help is provided, children can overcome the abuse and the impairments.

DOMESTIC VIOLENCE AS A HUMAN RIGHTS VIOLATION

Domestic violence is a human rights issue. Charlotte Bunch (1992) says, "The concept of human rights is one of the few moral visions ascribed to internationally" (p. 4). One would argue then that domestic violence violates this moral vision. Over the years it has been a challenge to view domestic violence as a human rights issue due to the cultural and sociological complexity of gender roles and dynamics in cultures across the globe.

A Brief History of Human Rights

In 1990, then-senator Joe Biden of Delaware introduced on the senate floor the Violence Against Women Act (VAWA). As a result of his steadfast and tenacious efforts, for the next 4 years he introduced victims to tell their stories. At the same time, the Committee on the Elimination of Discrimination Against Women (1992) and the Declaration of Elimination of Violence Against Women (1993) were introduced. In 1994, the Violence Against Women Act was passed. A national hotline for victims was finally established in this country in 1996. Although these efforts are admirable, many would argue it took us as a nation way too long to support victims of domestic violence.

Although there were many advocates in the United States who recognized the need for protection and support for women of abuse, many women still struggled with receiving the necessary support from law enforcement here in the United States. The Inter American Commission on Human Rights (IACHR) can be utilized to provide justice. One such case involved, Jessica Lenahan (formerly Gonzalez).

In 1999, Jessica's estranged husband abducted their three daughters, violating an existing restraining order. During the course of the abduction, Jessica met with law enforcement numerous times and did not receive the support she needed to enforce the restraining order against her estranged husband. Ultimately her daughters—ages 10, 9, and 7—died at the hands of their father.

After Jessica exhausted all opportunities via the U.S. judicial system, including meeting with law enforcement and finally ending with the U.S. Supreme Court, Jessica brought her case to the Inter American Commission on Human Rights in 2005. The IACHR offers an alternative channel for people to advocate for fundamental rights, social change, and institutional reform (Garcia-Rey, 2011).

Jessica's case was the first domestic violence survivor to introduce legal action against the United States for violating her and her daughters' human rights. On August 17, 2011, the Commission found the United States responsible for human rights violations. The recommendations made was for the United States to make changes to U.S. domestic violence laws and policies. See Sidebar 2.3 for more information on Jessica Gonzalez.

The Gonzales case was a landmark decision and framed domestic violence as a human rights violation and, in doing so, called in to question the United States' current practices and policies regarding supporting victims of domestic violence.

> **Sidebar 2.3**
>
> Below is more information on Jessica Gonzales and her devastating experience with domestic violence.
>
> - *Home Truth*—A documentary about Jessica Gonzales's experience with domestic violence and her pursuit for justice after the death of her three young daughters: http://www.hometruthfilm.com.
> - "*Castle Rock v. Gonzales*: Making the Court's Protection Real"—This website has an interview with Jessica Gonzales provided by the ACLU Women's Rights Project: https://www.aclu.org/other/castle-rock-v-gonzales-making-courts-protection-real?redirect=cpredirect/13212.
> - "*Gonzales vs. Castle Rock*: Supreme Court to Decide if Mother Can Sue Her Town and Its Police"—The following is the transcript from the show *60 Minutes* detailing Jessica Gonzales's case: https://www.cbsnews.com/news/gonzales-vs-castle-rock.

EFFECTS OF DOMESTIC VIOLENCE ON CHILDREN

Domestic violence or IPV adversely affects not only those being abused but also the children who witness the violence. In 1999, Jeff Edleson was one of a few who opened a scholarly discussion about the trauma experienced by children who witness domestic violence and its effects on the academic and cognitive development of these children. Edleson (1999a; 1999b) defines witnessing a violent event as being within visual range and seeing it occur; however, he also notes that while some children may witness the violence, most often children hear the violent event and experience its aftermath. These children have been called the "silent," "forgotten," and "unintended" victims of adult-on-adult domestic violence (Edleson, 1999a; 1999b).

When family violence occurs, children feel that they do not have a safe haven. In violent homes, it is typical that one parent is the terrifying aggressor and the other parent is the terrified victim; children have no refuge for protection. It has been said that domestic violence psychologically robs a child of both parents.

Children from violent homes come to school with various behaviors and emotions that can make it difficult for them to learn. It is often difficult for educators to discern the reasons behind children's behavioral and learning problems since family violence is frequently kept secret from school personnel (Massachusetts Advocates for Children, 2005). Furthermore, many myths have been perpetuated via media and in society in general that make a difficult for educators to truly recognize the effects domestic violence can have on children.

The Massachusetts Advocates for Children (2005) and Edleson (1999a) have found that between 3.3 million and 10 million children in the United States witness violence in their own homes each year. Still another survey conducted by the Massachusetts Department of Education, which was given to 450 students who attended alternative education programs in 11 school districts, found further indication that domestic violence is prevalent among school-aged children (Massachusetts Advocates for Children, 2005).

The results indicated that 90% of the students reported histories of trauma exposure, with a number of these students reporting exposure to more than one type of trauma. Of the students surveyed, 41% reported histories of family violence; 46% reported having been physically, emotionally, or sexually abused; and 39% reported neglect (Massachusetts Advocates for Children, 2005).

Most recently, the National Survey of Children's Exposure to Violence (NATSCEV) was conducted. It is the most comprehensive nationwide survey of the incidence and prevalence of children's exposure to violence to date, sponsored by the Office of Juvenile Justice and Delinquency Prevention (OJJDP) and the Centers for Disease Control and Prevention (CDC), and it found further startling statistics (Hamby et al., 2011).

One in four children (26%) were exposed to at least one form of family violence during their lifetimes (Hamby et al., 2011). Most youth exposed to family violence, including 90% of those exposed to IPV, saw the violence as opposed to hearing it or other indirect forms of exposure (Hamby et al., 2011). Children who live in a household where there is domestic violence are at a high risk for being abused themselves. An estimated 45% to 70% of children who witness domestic abuse are also physically abused (Holt et al., 2008).

Research reveals many lasting negative effects of domestic violence (Spath, 2003; Edelson, 1999a; 1999b; NACVAW, n.d.; Kearney, 2001). Traumatic experiences change children's expectations of the world and destroy the victim's fundamental assumptions about the safety and expectations of the world (Massachusetts Advocates for Children, 2005). As a result, children's safety and security of interpersonal life is redefined or changed (Massachusetts Advocates for Children, 2005).

Children may also have diminished self-worth or feel incapable of having a positive impact on the outside world (Massachusetts Advocates for Children, 2005; Kearney, 2001). Children witnessing domestic violence also may experience developmental delays or have increased behavioral and emotional problems (Spath, 2003; NACVAW, n.d.; MacKay, 2012; Kearney, 2001).

Children exposed to domestic violence often show symptoms in the areas of behavioral and emotional functioning, cognitive and school problems, and social relationships (Hughes et al., 2002; Holt et al., 2008). In addition to presenting learning challenges, children who witness domestic violence may become defiant or watch out for their siblings and/or pour themselves into activities that they love (Bancroft, 2004).

Further research suggests that children witnessing domestic violence may exhibit more aggressive and antisocial behaviors, withdrawal, fearful and inhibited behaviors, anxiety, depression, trauma-related symptoms, temperament problems, possible fear of authority, low tolerance for frustration, perfectionism, and lowered social competence than children who do not witness such violence (Holt et al., 2008; Phifer & McPherson, 2013; Cunningham & Baker, 2007; Hamby et al., 2011).

Additionally, many of the symptoms exhibited by children of domestic violence are also some of the same symptoms exhibited by children of substance-abusing parents (Ritter et al., 2002). Unfortunately, school-age maltreated children receive more disciplinary interventions, including suspensions for misconduct, than do non-maltreated children. It is important to note that suspensions and/or disciplinary actions may not be the appropriate intervention for every child. Each child reacts as an individual. There is neither one pattern of response nor a syndrome to sum up the impact of their experiences (Kearney, 2001; Hamby et al., 2011).

As children enter adolescence, they may recreate the abusive behaviors they witnessed as younger children. When adolescents begin to enter intimate relationships of their own, they may become abusers themselves. Rakovec-Felser (2014) report that male perpetrators are much more likely than others to have grown up in homes where adult domestic violence did occur and, thus, model the behavior they witnessed. Adolescents who witnessed domestic violence as children are more likely to abuse drugs and alcohol, run away from home, or commit other delinquent behaviors (NACVAW, n.d.).

Kearney (2001) and Visser and colleagues (2012) examined the relationship between parental alcohol abuse, family conflict, and adolescent experimentation with alcohol. They found that family conflict, adverse life events, and reduced family cohesion were better predictors of early adolescent experimentation with alcohol than was parental alcohol abuse (Kearney, 2001). The "silent," "forgotten," or "unintended" victims are at greater risk of becoming drug and alcohol abusers or violent abusers because of the domestic violence they witnessed as children and/or because they were abused themselves.

Other researchers point to the fact that different characteristics appear for boys and girls who have witnessed violence (Stagg et al., 1989; Ritter et al., 2002). Boys have been known to show more externalized problems like aggression and hostility. On the other hand, girls show more internalized problems such as depression (Rakovec-Felser, 2014; Stagg et al., 1989; Ritter et al., 2002). See sidebar 2.4 for further symptoms or signs of a child who has witnessed domestic violence.

Recognizing that a child may be witnessing domestic violence in the home or is a victim of domestic violence could be difficult for educators. Children have been "trained" that what happens in the home is a private family matter, and therefore they may not be willing to share. Teachers can observe behaviors and keep in mind that a child may be suffering from witnessing domestic violence.

Sidebar 2.4. Warning Signs of Exposure to Domestic Violence or IPV

Educators may immediately witness a child's behavior as a result of domestic violence, or behaviors may appear later. Every child is their own individual, and behaviors may be different as well. Culture must also be considered as another factor in the different ways children may react. Gender, too, plays a part in the type of behaviors that may be displayed. Lastly, age is another factor when considering the behaviors a child may exhibit. The following is a checklist by age:

- Children 5 and younger may exhibit the following behaviors:
  - regression—also, behaviors exhibited by younger children may appear like bed wetting, thumb sucking, and fear of the dark;
  - frequent tantrums;
  - clinging to caregivers;
  - changes in level of activity;
  - repeat events over and over in play and conversation;
  - difficulty sleeping;
  - frequent illnesses; and
  - somatic or psychosomatic complaints (aches and pains with no clear medical cause).

- Elementary school–age children (6–12 years) may exhibit the following behaviors:
  - difficulty paying attention;
  - fighting with peers and adults;
  - changes in school performance—may have difficulty or may work hard;
  - change in eating habits;
  - exhibiting external (aggression or hostility) or internal (withdrawn or depressed) behaviors;
  - parentified behaviors (takes on the role of a parent for younger siblings);
  - diminished cognitive skills; and
  - hypervigilance.

(continued)

> **Sidebar 2.4. continued**
>
> - Teenagers (13–18 years) may exhibit the following behaviors:
>   - not following rules;
>   - delinquency;
>   - engaging in risky behaviors (drugs, alcohol, and sexual activity);
>   - aggressive behaviors;
>   - becoming withdrawn;
>   - nightmares;
>   - running away from home;
>   - complaining of not feeling well or being tired;
>   - diminished cognitive skills; and
>   - hypervigilance.
>
> As with a lot of these signs, some may be "normal" child development. Collaborating with counseling professionals and/or outside community agencies can also help provide further insight regarding the ways to best support the child in the classroom.

A teacher's role is to teach, and so understanding how a child is affected cognitively and behaviorally and then knowing the proper strategies to implement are part of that role. In the following chapters, further cognitive and behavior struggles are uncovered for children of trauma, and some strategies that can be used to best support our youngest victims are provided.

REFERENCES

Babcock, J. C., & La Taillade, J. J. (2000). Evaluating interventions for men who batter. In J. P. Vincent & E. N. Jouriles (Eds.), *Domestic violence: Guidelines for research-informed practice* (pp. 37–77). Jessica Kingsley.

Bancroft, L. (2004). *Helping your children heal the wounds of witnessing abuse.* Berkley Books.

Black, M. C., Basile, K. C., Breiding, M. J., Smith, S. G., Walters, M. L., Merrick, M. T., & Stevens, M. R. (2011). The National Intimate Partner and Sexual Violence Survey (NISVS): 2010 summary report. Centers for Disease Control and Prevention.

Bohall, G., Bautista, M. J., & Musson, S. (2016). Intimate partner violence and the Duluth Model: An examination of the model and recommendations for future research and practice. *Journal of Family Violence, 31*, 1029–1033.

Breiding, M. J., Basile, K. C., Smith, S. G., Black, M. C., & Mahendra, R. R. (2015). *Intimate partner violence surveillance: Uniform definitions and recommended data elements, version 2.0.* National Center for Injury Prevention and Control, Centers for Disease Control and Prevention.

Buckley, H., Holt, S., & Whelan, S. (2007). Listen to me! Children's experiences of domestic violence. *Child Abuse Review, 16*, 296–310.

Bunch, C. (1992). Violence against women is a violation of human rights. *Women in Law Development in Africa News*.

Burge, S. K., Katerndahl, D. A., Wood, R. C., Becho, J., Ferrer, R. L., & Talamantes, M. (2015). Using complexity science to examine three dynamic patterns of intimate partner violence. *Families, Systems and Health, 34*(1), 4–14.

Centers for Disease Control. (2017). *Intimate partner violence: Definitions.* https://www.cdc.gov/violenceprevention/intimatepartnerviolence/definitions.html.

Cunningham, A., & Baker, L. (2007). *Little eyes, little ears: How violence against a mother shapes children as they grow.* Center for Children and Families in the Justice System. http://publications.gc.ca/collections/collection_2007/phac-aspc/HP20-5-2007E.pdf

Edelson, J. L. (1999a). Children's witnessing of adult domestic violence. *Journal of Interpersonal Violence, 14*, 839–870.

Edelson, J. L. (1999b). The overlap between child maltreatment and woman battering. *Violence Against Women, 5*, 134–154.

Exner-Cortens, D., Eckenrode, J., Bunge, J., & Rothman, E. (2017). Revictimization after adolescent dating violence in a matched, national sample of youth. *Journal of Adolescent Health, 60*(2), 176–183.

Finkelhor, D., Shattuck, A., Turner, H. A., & Hamby, S. L. (2014). Trends in children's exposure to violence, 2003–2011. *JAMA Pediatrics, 168*(6), 540–546.

Garcia-Rey, P. (2011). *Domestic violence as a human rights violation.* American Civil Liberties Union. https://www.aclu.org/blog/womens-rights/violence-against-women/domestic-violence-human-rights-violation

Hamby, S., Finkelhor, D., Turner, H., & Ormrod, R. (2011). *Children's exposure to intimate partner violence and other family violence* [Bulletin]. https://www.ncjrs.gov/pdffiles1/ojjdp/232272.pdf

Holden, G. W. (2003). Children exposed to domestic violence and child abuse: Terminology and taxonomy. *Clinical Child and Family Psychology Review, 6*, 151–160.

Holt, S., Buckley, H., & Whelan, S. (2008). The impact of exposure to domestic violence on children and young people: A review of the literature. *Child Abuse & Neglect, 32*, 797–810.

Hughes, H. M., Graham-Bermann, S., & Gruber, G. (2002). Resilience in children exposed to domestic violence. In S. A. Graham-Bermann & J. L. Edleson (Eds.), *Domestic violence in the lives of children.* (pp. 67–90). American Psychological Association.

Kearney, M. (2001). The role of teachers in helping children of domestic violence. In *Teachers' Resource: Child Abuse and Domestic Violence* (pp. 17–22). Association for Childhood Education International.

MacKay, L. (2012). Trauma and Bowen Family Systems Theory: Working with adults who were abused as children. Australian and New Zealand Journal of Family Therapy, 33(3), 232–241.

Massachusetts Advocates for Children, the Hale and Dorr Legal Services Center of Harvard Law School, & Task Force on Children Affected by Domestic Violence. (2005). *Helping traumatized children learn.* http://www.massadvocates.org/helping_traumatized_children_learn

Murray, C. E. (2006). Controversy, constraints, and context: Understanding family violence through family systems theory. *The Family Journal: Counseling and Therapy for Couples and Families, 14*(3), 234–239.

National Advisory Council on Violence Against Women and the Violence Against Women Office. (n.d.). Intervention and prevention for children and youth. In *Toolkit to End Violence Against Women* (chap. 9). http://toolkit.ncjrs.org/vawo_9.html

Pence, E., & Paymar, M. (1993). *Education groups for men who batter: The Duluth model.* Springer.

Phifer, L. W., & McPherson, D. A. (2013). Developmental differences in response to trauma. In E. Rossen & R. Hull (Eds.), *Supporting and educating traumatized students: A guide for school-based professionals.* Oxford University Press.

Rakovec-Felser, Z. (2014). Domestic violence and abuse in intimate relationship from public health perspective. *Health Psychology Research, 2*(3). https://doi.org/10.4081/hpr.2014.1821

Ritter, J., Stewart, M., Bernet, C., & Coe, M. (2002). Effects of childhood exposure to familial alcoholism and family violence on adolescent substance use, conduct problems, and self-esteem. *Journal of Traumatic Stress, 15,* 113–122.

Saunders, D. G. (2001). Developing guidelines for domestic violence offender programs: What can we learn from related fields and current research? *Journal of Aggression, Maltreatment, and Trauma, 5,* 235–248.

Smith, S. G., Chen, J., Basile, K. C., Gilbert, L. K., Merrick, M. T., Patel, N., Walling, M., & Jain, A. (2017). *The National Intimate Partner and Sexual Violence Survey (NISVS): 2010–2012 state report.* National Center for Injury Prevention and Control, Centers for Disease Control and Prevention.

Snyder, R. L. (2019). *No visible bruises: What we don't know about domestic violence can kill us.* Bloomsbury Publishing.

Spath, R. (2003). Child protection professionals identifying domestic violence indicators: Implications for social work education. *Journal of Social Work Education, 39,* 497–518.

Stagg, V., Wills, G. D., & Howell, M. (1989). Psychopathology in early childhood witnesses of family violence. *Topics in Early Childhood Special Education, 9,* 73–87.

Sun, J., Patel, F., Rose-Jacobs, R., Frank, D. A., Black, M. M., & Chilton, M. (2017). Mothers' adverse childhood experiences and their young children's development. *American Journal of Preventive Medicine, 53*(6), 882–891.

Visser, L., de Winter, A. F., & Reijineveld, S. A. (2012). The parent-child relationship and adolescent alcohol use: a systematic review of longitudinal studies. Bio Med Central Public Health, 12, 1–16.

3

Impact of Trauma on Children Across Developmental Stages

> This chapter will provide:
> - an overview of child development theories and theorists; and
> - the ways trauma can affect children at various developmental stages.

CHILD DEVELOPMENT AND MATURATION OF SKILLS

When discussing various developmental stages, it's important for us to recognize that every child will move at their own pace, and it's the mastery of the skills or mastery of specific developmental milestones that is important to acknowledge. As we begin to explore the various theorists below, remember to keep in mind these stages are average ages and that each child develops at their own speed.

How can trauma affect a child's development? Trauma may inhibit a child from reaching a milestone within a particular timeframe. Children could regress within certain developmental stages. Being familiar with developmental stages and the major child development theories can help educators pinpoint atypical development and then provide interventions to further support developmental growth.

Theorists agree that there are times of maturation in a child's life that enable children to learn new skills more easily (Prior & Glaser, 2006; Erikson, 1963; 1968; 1959/1994; Piaget, 1929). For example, babies and toddlers learn language more freely than do older children. Environmental stimuli also support the maturation of skills for babies and toddlers. A loving, nurturing environment provides children with the support and tools to thrive and grow as they learn new skills.

Researchers (Bowlby, 1969; Prior & Glaser, 2006) have uncovered the importance of a secure attachment bond (otherwise known as attachment theory) between the "principal figure in their environment, namely his mother" (Bowlby, 1969, p. 180). Children of neglect or abuse may have difficulty receiving the needed environmental stimuli during critical periods, which can hamper their growth physically, emotionally, and cognitively. Streeck-Fischer and van der Kolk (2000) state that the more exposure children have to different risk factors, the less resilient they will be. However, a caregiver who provides support and commitment will offer the greatest source of resilience for the child.

Language acquisition could be difficult for children if they are living in a neglectful or abusive home environment. Because acquiring language is a critical period and development may be delayed if the child's home environment is compromised, it is believed this inability to develop is not permanent and there are strategies and supports that can be provided to support the child (strategies and "tools" will be provided in later chapters).

CHILD DEVELOPMENT THEORISTS

For those of you working closely with children, the following theorists may already be familiar to you, but for others this may be your first introduction. If this is the case, further research and education may be necessary if you choose to learn more regarding each theory. See sidebar 3.1 for additional internet resources addressing some of the subsequent child development theorists.

Sidebar 3.1

The following are additional internet resources you may choose to use to educate yourself further about the child development theorists presented in chapter 3.

1. *Schemas, Assimilation, and Accommodation*—This is a video presented by Khan Academy that reviews Piaget's cognitive development theory including the three terms *schema, assimilation,* and *accommodation*. Other videos are available, including Piaget's stages of cognitive development: https://www.khanacademy.org/test-prep/mcat/processing-the-environment/cognition/v/schemas-assimilation-and-accommodation-2
2. Pathways Inc., a nonprofit organization, offers free child development information to empower parents and health professionals. This link provides checklists that can be used to track a child's development through 6 years of age: https://pathways.org/topics-of-development/milestones/checklists

3. *Child Development Theorists* is a video that provides information regarding 15 major development philosophies from the following theorists as well as others: Lev Vygotsky, Jean Piaget, Erik Erikson, Abraham Maslow, John Bowlby, Lawrence Kohlberg, and Howard Gardner: https://www.learningzonexpress.com/child-development-theorists-dvd.html
4. This next video reviews Erikson's theory of psychosocial development and the eight stages an individual passes through during their lifetime: https://www.youtube.com/watch?v=aYCBdZLCDBQ
5. In the 1980s at the University of California–Berkeley, Urie Bronfenbrenner provided a talk titled "The Developing Ecology of Human Development: Paradigm Lost or Paradigm Regained?" https://www.youtube.com/watch?time_continue=2&v=xaQHgVaeKrc

Erik Erikson

Erik Erikson is best recognized for his theory regarding how people's sense of identity or personality develops across the lifespan (Erikson, 1963; 1968; 1959/1994). This theory is known as Psychosocial Theory because it combines how people develop beliefs psychologically with how they progress within society or a larger community of people. He notes that there are conflicts at each stage that need to be resolved in order to promote healthy psychosocial development. His developmental progression includes the following stages and ages and was conceived as the sequential reorganization of Ego and character structures:

1. trust versus mistrust (birth to 1 year);
2. autonomy versus shame and doubt (1–3 years);
3. initiative versus guilt (4–5 years);
4. industry versus inferiority (6–11 years);
5. Ego identity versus role confusion (12–20 years);
6. intimacy versus isolation (20–24 years);
7. generativity versus stagnation (25–64 years); and
8. integrity versus despair (65 years to death). (Erikson, 1963; 1968; 1959/1994)

Erikson's theory involves the mastery and types of stimulation needed at each stage of psychosocial development to ensure the child becomes a productive and well-adjusted member of society. If the stimulation at each level does not occur and the conflict of the stage is not resolved, potential problems and developmental delays could ensue. As a result, these could become potential roots of later health issues and pathology. Erikson describes that experiences later in life can heal or ameliorate problems in early childhood. This aspect is particularly significant when we consider childhood trauma because, as we discussed in chapter 1, current research has informed us of the detrimental effects Adverse Childhood Experiences can have on later health and pathology. Table 3.1 provides the virtue gained at each psychosocial conflict stage and the potential outcomes of success or failure at each conflict level.

Table 3.1. Erikson's Psychosocial Conflict Stage, Psychosocial Virtue and Outcome

Psychosocial Crisis or Conflict	Age and Stage	Psychosocial Virtue or Resolution	Environmental Focus/ Influence	Outcome
Trust versus mistrust	Birth to 1 year infancy	Hope	Mother and other caregivers	Children develop trust as caregivers provide reliable care and affection. A lack of appropriate care will lead to mistrust.
Autonomy versus shame and doubt	1–3 years early childhood	Will	Parents	Children develop a sense of independence and the need to have personal control over physical skills (i.e., dressing and feeding). Success leads to feelings of autonomy and failure can result in a sense of shame and doubt.
Initiative versus guilt	4–5 years preschool	Purpose	Family	Children need to begin to assert control and power over their environment, and success will lead to a sense of purpose. Children exerting too much power experience disapproval and ultimately guilt.
Industry versus inferiority	6–11 years middle childhood	Competence	Neighborhood; school	Children learn to cope with social and academic demands. Success will lead to a sense of competence, while failure can result in a sense of inferiority.

Psychosocial Crisis or Conflict	Age and Stage	Psychosocial Virtue or Resolution	Environmental Focus/ Influence	Outcome
Ego identity versus role confusion	12–20 years adolescence	Fidelity	Peer groups or role models	Teens need to develop a sense of self. Success leads teens to be true to themselves, while failure leads to role confusion and a weak sense of self.
Intimacy versus isolation	20–34 years young adulthood	Love	Friends; partners; lover; spouse	Young adults need to form intimate relationships. Success will lead to strong relationships, while failure will result in loneliness and isolation.
Generativity versus stagnation	35–64 years middle adulthood	Care	Household; workmates	Adults need to nurture and care for things that will outlast them. Some will have children, while others will create positive change that benefits the greater good. Success leads to pride and a feeling of accomplishment, while failure may result in shallow involvement in the world.
Integrity versus despair	65 years to death old age	Wisdom	"Humankind" (all humans)	Older adults need to look back on life and feel a sense of fulfillment, and success will lead to a feeling of wisdom. Failure can result in regret and despair.

Adapted from Erikson (1994).

Jean Piaget

Jean Piaget, a Swiss psychologist, crafted a theory known as the Cognitive-Developmental Stage Theory (Piaget, 1929). This theory describes how children's way of thinking develops as they interact with the world around them. According to Piaget (1929; 1965/1995; 1954) and Piaget and Cook (1952), children learn about the world around them as they play and explore.

Piaget's theory includes four stages: the sensorimotor, preoperational, concrete operational, and formal operational (Piaget, 1929). During the sensorimotor stage, which is from birth to about 2 years of age, the child will begin to understand the world through their motor abilities like touch, taste, vision, and movement. Infants are extremely egocentric and have no concept that the world exists separate from their point of view and experience (Piaget, 1965/1995).

In order for infants to understand that objects continue to exist even when they are unseen, infants first develop a mental representation of the object, what Piaget referred to as *schema* (Piaget, 1965/1995). Schema is a cognitive framework or concept that helps to organize and interpret information about the world. As a child grows older and learns more information, schemas will enlarge and become more involved. Through processes known as assimilation and accommodation, new categories develop, and existing categories expand and can even completely change their current schemas. (See sidebar 3.2 for more information of how schema, assimilation, and accommodation can be equated to a filing cabinet.)

During the preoperational stage, from 2–7 years of age, children are thinking at a symbolic level but are not yet using cognitive operations. Language begins and explodes during this stage. This means the child cannot use logic or transform, combine, or separate ideas (Piaget, 1965/1995; Piaget & Cook, 1952). During the end of this stage, children can mentally represent events and objects and engage in symbolic or pretend play.

Concrete operational is the stage (during ages 7–11) that children begin to gain the ability to think logically to solve problems and to organize

---

Sidebar 3.2. Piaget's Schema Theory

Piaget (1952) defines schema as "a cohesive a cohesive, repeatable action sequence possessing component actions that are tightly interconnected and governed by a core meaning" (p. 7). Schema allows us to build mental representations of everything in our world—it's a way of organizing knowledge. In teaching my college-level students, I equate schema to a filing cabinet in our brain. Each file is a different "schema" or thing. One file might be zoo; another file related to zoo might be tigers but has specific information regarding just tigers.

Two related terms to schema are assimilation and accommodation. Intellectual growth occurs as we adapt or adjust to our world through assimilation and accommodation (Wadsworth, 2004; Piaget, 1952). Assimilation uses our existing schema to incorporate a new object or situation, whereas accommodation occurs when the existing schema does not work, and it needs to be changed to accommodate the new object or situation. An example of assimilation would be when a child learns that their mother is Mommy and therefore calls their grandmother, another female, Mommy. The child is corrected, and it is explained that the other female is Grandmom, modifying schema and thereby using accommodation.

information they learn (Piaget, 1954). At this stage, they are only able to consider concrete information, due to their abstract thinking not being well developed yet. Children during this stage, unlike previous stages, see a decrease in egocentrism. While children in the previous stages have difficulty taking the perspective of others, in this stage we see children able to think about things the way others see them.

Formal operational, which begins at age 11 and lasts until adulthood, is the fourth and final stage of Piaget's theory (Piaget & Cook, 1952). Thinking becomes more advanced and theoretical concepts and abstract thinking are more sophisticated. Skills like logical thought, deductive reasoning, and systematic planning emerge during this stage (Piaget, 1965/1995).

Jean Piaget's work is very well known within the fields of psychology and education and has made a huge impact on the way we view child development. It has helped many to understand child development, and his theories have provided profound information about the way children think and their mental development. Piaget's work regarding children's development has been used repeatedly to develop educational programming and instructional strategies (Piaget, 1929; 1965/1995; 1954).

Urie Bronfenbrenner

Urie Bronfenbrenner developed the Ecological Systems Theory of child development. Bronfenbrenner's (1979; 1994) theory explains how a child's environment affects their growth and development. The path of development is a result of the influences of a person's surroundings—for example, parents, friends, school, work, culture, and so on. He conceptualizes four ecological systems: the microsystem, mesosystem, exosystem, and macrosystem.

The microsystem is the small, immediate environment within which a child lives. The immediate relationships or organizations included here are the child's immediate family or caregivers and their school or daycare (Bronfenbrenner, 1979; 1994). The way these members interact with the child will have an effect on how the child grows and develops. Therefore, the more nurturing, encouraging, and positive these relationships are, the better the child will grow and develop.

The mesosystem describes how the different parts of a child's microsystem work together for the sake of the child. If a child's caretakers are involved in the child's school, such as attending parent-teacher conferences, this will help guarantee the child's overall, positive growth (Bronfenbrenner, 1979; 1994). Conversely, if members of the microsystem are not working together or disagree on aspects of the child's upbringing, this will hinder the child's growth.

The exosystem level includes the other people and places that the child may not have direct interactions with but that may still have a large effect on the child. Some examples could include parents' workplaces, extended family members, the neighborhood, and so on. If a parent loses their job, it could have a negative effect on the child, as the parent may not be able to pay rent or buy necessities like groceries. In contrast, if a parent receives a promotion and a raise at work, this could have a positive effect on the child because the parents are better able to provide for the child's needs.

The final level is the macrosystem, which is the largest all-encompassing set of people and things to a child. This includes societal beliefs, economy, wars, cultural norms, and so on, which can either positively or negatively influence an individual's development (Bronfenbrenner, 1979; 1994).

CHILD DEVELOPMENT AND TRAUMA

The theorists we explored above made it clear that as children grow and change from birth, their ability to think and to get along with others is a growth process as well. To be successful adults, children need to be nurtured and educated regarding the skills necessary to work well with others. We use chronological age to determine developmental level and gauge typical as well as atypical behavior.

The following section will explore trauma from a developmental stance. It is important to note that as children develop, there is wide range of normal developmental markers, and therefore, children are not always developmentally similar in their progression. Furthermore, responses to trauma differ from person to person as well. It is important for educators and anyone working with children to react to each child individually given their developmental stage. Further support for educators may need to be sought from professionals who work closely with children since trauma can also lead to other psychological diagnoses like social anxiety disorder and post-traumatic stress disorder (Bishop et al., 2014).

Early Childhood (Infancy through Preschool)

As we learned from Piaget (1929; 1954) and Erikson (1959/1994), during infancy through preschool age, in a nurturing environment with positive caregivers, the child is learning to trust others, gaining autonomy, and developing self-confidence for exploration and active play with others. Babies have little awareness of self and cannot discriminate between cues and needs. This awareness of self begins to develop. The infant learns to trust their caregiver and to communicate their needs, effectively forming an attachment and bond. In an unsupportive environment or with unresponsive caregivers, the child will have difficulty trusting adults and may fear others. Furthermore, communication may be limited, as various communicative strategies were not learned or were limited in scope.

Object permanence, first studied by Piaget (1954), is the idea that a child can hold an image of an object in his mind even when it is out of sight. Prior to about 7 months of age, if a toy falls under the couch and is no longer in view, the baby will believe the toy no longer exists. Separation anxiety can begin to develop usually around 7 months (but for most babies it may develop between 10 and 18 months) because it is at this time that the infant begins to realize that when a parent or caregiver is out of sight, she/he still exists.

Another term coined by Piaget (1954), related to object permanence and considered to be its emotional equivalence, is *object constancy*. *Object constancy* is the ability to maintain an emotional bond with others even when there is distance or disagreement. Object constancy allows the child to hold the image of a caring, supportive adult in mind. Being able to hold a comforting image of the caregiver's love allows the child to grow developmentally and emotionally.

Unfortunately, this concept is difficult to achieve for many maltreated children who live in unpredictable and inconsistent environments. Children living in homes where there is abuse and domestic violence are uncertain if their caregiver is going to commit violent acts. It is extremely difficult for children to develop object constancy when the image they have in their mind may be of a person who is not comforting.

As the child moves into the toddler stage, Erikson (1959/1994) describes the psychosocial developmental task as autonomy versus shame and guilt. Toddlers are exploring their world and begin to develop a sense of agency, independence, or autonomy. This belief of autonomy leads them to realize they have an impact on the world. Sorrels (2015) notes that a child's sense of autonomy is a strong predictor of academic success and positive adjustment to school as the child begins their education. Furthermore, "Children who successfully negotiate this stage of development generally acquire a strong sense of self, a healthy independence, and the ability to comply with reasonable consistency to the appropriate expectation of family and school" (Sorrels, 2015, p. 153).

At this stage, toddlers begin to use the word *no* as a declaration of independence and the recognition of self. A child who has experienced trauma will have profound difficulty in the healthy development of autonomy. A child of trauma may lack a consistent and safe caregiver to help the child define himself/herself. Children may have difficulty with self-regulation, have difficulty navigating in group settings, demonstrate aggressive behaviors, have fewer social relationships, and have difficulty during periods of transition (Sorrels, 2015; Wiebler, 2013; Blaustein & Kinniburgh, 2010).

Another tendency for young children is egocentrism. At this early age, toddlers are not able to understand different points of view. For example, if a child sees a caregiver upset, they may give the caregiver their favorite stuffed animal, reasoning that what comforts the child can also provide relief to the adult. Egocentric thinking can also cause the child to feel responsible or accept blame if something bad happens. This occurrence can also be known as *magical thinking*. Magical thinking is the belief that what a child wishes or expects can affect what really happens (Wiebler, 2013).

Agency and independence continue into the preschool years. Preschool children continue to explore the world and test the boundaries around them. Their interpretation of their world is concrete, and time is not yet understood at this level. Preschoolers are "tuned into structure, repetition and security," as these can all be comforting for their emotionality (Blaustein & Kinniburgh, 2010, p. 12). At this age, children like to reread the same story or watch their favorite television show over and over.

Developmentally, children at this age enjoy exploring their world. A child living in an unpredictable, unsafe, or stressed environment will lack the ability to explore their world (Streeck-Fischer & van der Kolk, 2000). Since children of trauma may experience an erratic caregiver and environment, their exploration can be impacted. For instance, they may explore an environment that could be dangerous if their caregiver is unstable or negligent.

Conversely, a child may stay close to the unpredictable caregiver because they are afraid of their environment. Not only is exploration impacted, but agency is as well. The child in this type of environment will have less control, less impact, and less understanding of their world (Blaustein & Kinniburgh, 2010). The loss of structure and safety will lead preschool children to need strategies to cope with their anxiety.

Teachers may notice other behavioral and cognitive signs that point to the fact a preschool child has been impacted by trauma. Regression in toileting, feeding, and dressing skills may be noticed (Cunningham & Baker, 2007). The child may have difficulty "relaxing" and be in a constant state of hyperarousal or a constant state of fear. Crying often is not uncommon. Some children may destroy materials, be aggressive toward peers, and/or use inappropriate language. Preschool children may use play to act out the traumatic or adverse experience.

Elementary-Aged Students

As Bronfenbrenner (1994) notes in describing the microsystem and mesosystem, children benefit from positive caregivers and interactions between their various environments like school, community, and peer groups. During middle childhood, as children expand their worlds beyond their immediate family, peers and school are extremely important in shaping the child's world and are a basis of modeling support and acceptance (Wiebler, 2013). Peers can either support and accept each other or they can be a source of great despair and contribute to the child's adverse or traumatic experience. This aligns closely with Bronfenbrenner's (1994) theory about the ways the microsystem and mesosystem can positively or negatively affect an individual's growth and development.

Children during this developmental stage begin to produce and create a sense of pride and ownership. As we learned from Erikson (1963; 1968; 1959/1994), during the industry versus inferiority stage, their schoolwork builds confidence, and they begin to master new skills. Piaget's (1954) assimilation and accommodation are prevalent as children learn new material and begin to assimilate and accommodate this new information into their already-existing schemas. Furthermore, concrete information is relied on for meaning making, as abstract thinking does not fully materialize until the end of this stage.

If trauma or adverse experiences exist, children will demonstrate impairments in social and cognitive development. More specifically, children of trauma may have difficulty regulating behaviors, including controlling impulses, difficulty concentrating, interpersonal relationship struggles, and short-term memory and executive functioning complications (Cunningham & Baker, 2007). Loss of early exploration and failure to develop a sense of agency may begin to impact children's capacity to perform and sustain performance in the school setting (Shonk and Cicchetti, 2001).

During the latter half of this stage, early signs of helplessness and hopelessness may emerge (Kim & Cicchetti, 2006). Hopelessness can also be witnessed in the child's difficulty in expressing their feelings. They will have a hard time linking the correct adjective with how they are feeling. Additionally, some students may not be able to manage their feelings and therefore become physically aggressive. Their aggression may be aimed at the perceived source of trauma, the adults who fail to protect them, or even their classmates. There is a plethora of emotional, social, and cognitive difficulties that could further exist. They are listed in figure 3.1.

- Excessive worry
- Anxiety
- Emotional numbing
- Withdrawal, isolation from others
- Restlessness
- Learning difficulties

*noncompliance
*bullying behaviors
*hyperactive
*shut down

Figure 3.1 Behaviors children of trauma may exhibit. *Source:* Colleen Lelli

Secondary-Aged Students or Adolescence

Adolescence is a period of great transition in all areas, including physical, cognitive, and social development. During this stage, Erikson notes that adolescents are formulating their identity or developing a sense of self. They are trying to find their place in society and exploring questions like, "Who am I?" and "Where do I fit?" During this time as teens are defining themselves, they may experiment and try and discard various roles as they continue to seek their identity. Teens do seem self-absorbed or egocentric at this level, but it's less about lack of awareness of the outside world (like in infancy and early childhood) and more about how the outside world may be viewing and focusing on them (Blaustein & Kinniburgh, 2010).

As a normal adolescent behavior, teens begin to question authority and separate from the caregiving system while turning to peer groups for acceptance, belonging, and information. In healthy adolescent development, the caregivers are available as needed for the teen during times of questioning and distress.

Teens are learning to regulate interactions with others. Teens of trauma will have an even more difficult time regulating their interactions with others and may disconnect from relationships and peer interactions. "The belief that others are examining them as intently as they are examining themselves can lead to a painful self-consciousness and crystallization of a negative self-identity" (Blaustein & Kinniburgh, 2010, p. 16). Bronfenbrenner's (1979; 1994) Ecological Systems Theory directly aligns with this thinking, as he explained the importance of interactions with others in a child's development.

Some adolescents who suffer trauma will try to over-control situations and throw themselves into their schoolwork, while others may resort to such behaviors as cutting classes, engaging in sexual activities, or abusing substances (Kendall-Tackett et al., 1993). Teens' lack of impulse control and inappropriate behaviors are not tolerated by adults, as the expectation is that they should have learned to regulate their behaviors by this age. Teens who have suffered trauma in their childhood may not have had the opportunities to obtain these skills due to being in a constant state of hyperarousal and in survival mode. Teens may also process events through discussion or writing activities (Wiebler, 2013).

The information presented in this chapter was meant to provide the reader with a brief background of the ways trauma can affect a child across the developmental lifespan. When working with children, it's important to have an understanding of typical development so that atypical development and behaviors can be addressed, and proper interventions can better support students involved in traumatic experiences.

REFERENCES

Bishop, M., Rosenstein, D., Bakelaar, S., & Seedat, S. (2014). An analysis of early developmental trauma in social anxiety disorder and posttraumatic stress disorder. *Annals of General Psychiatry, 13*, 16. doi:10.1186/1744-859X-13-16

Blaustein, M., & Kinniburgh, K. (2010). *Treating traumatic stress in children and adolescents.* Guilford Press.

Bowlby, J. (1969). *Attachment and loss* (vol. 1). Basic Books.

Bronfenbrenner, U. (1979). *The ecology of human development.* Harvard University Press.

Bronfenbrenner, U. (1994). Ecological models of human development. *Readings on the Development of Children, 2*(1), 37–43.

Cunningham, A., & Baker, L. (2007). *Little eyes, Little ears: How violence against a mother shapes children as they grow.* Center for Children and Families in the Justice System.

Erikson, E. H. (1963). *Childhood and society.* Norton.

Erikson, E. H. (1968). *Identity, youth, and crisis.* Norton.

Erikson, E. H. (1994). *Identity and the life cycle.* Norton. (Original work published 1959)

Kendall-Tackett, K. A., Williams, L. M., & Finkelhor, D. (1993). Impact of sexual abuse on children: A review and synthesis of recent empirical studies. *Psychological Bulletin, 113,* 164–180.

Kim, J., & Cicchetti, D. (2006). Longitudinal trajectories of self-system processes and depressive symptoms among maltreated and normal treated children. *Child Development, 77*(3), 624–639.

Piaget, J. (1929). *The child's concept of the world.* Routledge & Kegan Paul.

Piaget, J. (1954). *The construction of reality in a child.* Abingdon, Oxon: Routledge.

Piaget, J. (1995). Egocentric thought and sociocentric thought. In *Sociological studies* (L. Smith, Trans.; pp. 270–286). Routledge. (Original work published 1965)

Piaget, J., & Cook, M. T. (1952). *The origins of intelligence in children.* International University Press.

Prior, V., & Glaser, D. (2006). *Understanding attachment and attachment disorders: Theory, evidence and practice.* Jessica Kingsley Publishers.

Shonk, S. M., & Cicchetti, D. (2001). Maltreatment, competency deficits, and risk for academic and behavioral maladjustment. *Developmental Psychology, 37*, 3–17.

Sorrels, B. (2015). *Reaching and teaching children exposed to trauma.* Gryphon House Inc.

Streeck-Fischer, A., & van der Kolk, B. A. (2000). Down will come baby, cradle and all: Diagnostic and therapeutic implications of chronic trauma on child development. *Australian and New Zealand Journal of Psychiatry, 34,* 903–918.

Wadsworth, B. J. (2004). *Piaget's theory of cognitive and affective development: Foundations of constructivism.* Longman Publishing.

Wiebler, L. R. (2013). Developmental differences in response to trauma. In E. Rossen & R. Hull (Eds.), *Supporting and educating traumatized students: A guide for school-based professionals.* Oxford University Press.

4

Impact of Trauma and the Interventions for Children's Language and Memory

This chapter will:
- define expressive and receptive language and the impact trauma may have on a child's development of these skills;
- provide strategies to support educators, counselors, and/or parents as they encourage the development of a child's expressive and receptive language skills;
- describe the impact of trauma on a child's short- and long-term memory; and
- offer strategies to provide educators, counselors, and/or parents as they scaffold a child's memory.

Recent research provides us with the ways stress and trauma can impact learning, memory and language and the ways the brain is affected (Sylvestre et al., 2015; Stevens et al., 2017; Samuelson, 2011). With the use of brain imaging, studies have shown activation of the pre-frontal cortex and increased activation in the amygdala during exposure to trauma-salient stimuli (Donegan, 2003; Minzenberg, 2008).

As a result, we are positioned now more than ever as educators to support children of trauma in the classroom. This chapter investigates how exposure to violence and trauma hampers the development of both expressive and receptive language and the impact on memory. Finally, strategies that can be implemented in the classroom are explored.

DEFINING EXPRESSIVE AND RECEPTIVE LANGUAGE

Language is a cognitive process that involves the ability to understand and use language to deliver or decipher a message. Expressive and receptive language are the two areas that relate to both the delivery and the deciphering of a message or messages within a conversation.

Expressive language is the use of words, sentences, gestures, and writing to convey a message. Expressive language is important because it allows a person to express their needs, thoughts, and ideas so that interactions with others can occur. To develop positive expressive language skills, some necessary prerequisites include understanding of language or receptive language skills; attention and concentration; pre-language skills like gestures, facial expressions, and eye contact; motivation or desire to communicate with others; and an understanding of pragmatics or the use of language in social situations.

Receptive language is the ability to understand or comprehend words and language; it allows a person to interpret and respond appropriately to experiences that they confront in their lives. To develop positive receptive language skills, some of the following are necessary prerequisites, including attention and concentration; pre-language skills like gestures, facial expressions, and eye contact; socials skills and reciprocal interaction with others; and play skills.

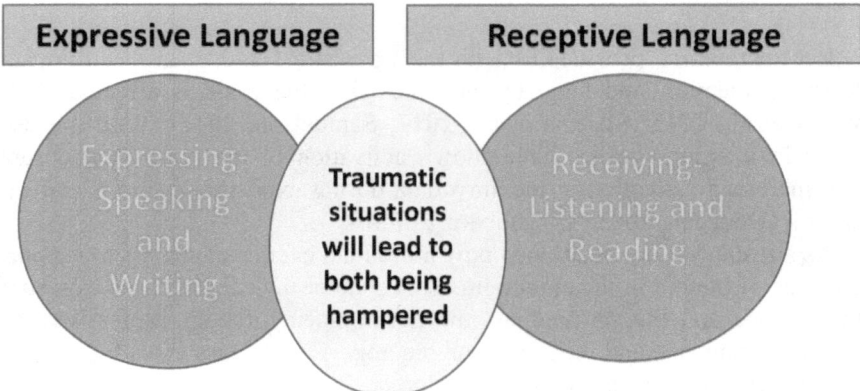

Figure 4.1   The impact of trauma on expressive and receptive language. *Source:* Colleen Lelli

IMPACT ON LANGUAGE

Sylvestre and colleagues (2015) conducted a meta-analysis exploring the language skills (expressive language, receptive language, and pragmatics) of children who have experienced abuse and/or neglect compared with the language skills of children who have not experienced these traumas. It was found that children who have experienced abuse and/or neglect are delayed when compared to children who have not experienced abuse and/or neglect. This study highlights the importance of early detection of language difficulties of children who have experienced abuse and/or neglect.

Further findings suggest that the younger the child, the more of an impact abuse and neglect will have on language (Sylvestre et al., 2015; Craig, 2008; van der Kolk, 2014). Deficits in language development have also been observed in vocabulary, fluency, listening, social discourse, and symbolism (Yehuda, 2005). With early detection, proper interventions can be employed to encourage children's language development.

As previously discussed in chapter 3, we know that language development blossoms for children when a supportive caregiver provides multiple opportunities for language exposure. A positive home environment is ideal for language growth, and children of trauma and/or abuse or neglect will suffer immensely in all areas of development without the proper support. In the sections that follow, we will explore the impact trauma can have on language development.

Impact on Expressive Language, Receptive Language, and Brain Functioning

Bessel van der Kolk (2014) and his team used functional magnetic resonance imaging (fMRI) to study the brain while people recounted their traumatic experiences. For the first time, they could "watch the brain as it processed memories, sensations and emotions and begin to map the circuits of the mind" (van der Kolk, 2014, p. 39). One of the most surprising and helpful findings was the effects trauma can have on an area of the brain known as Broca's area.

Broca's area is the area of the brain located in the lower portion of the left frontal lobe. It is responsible for speech or expressive language and functions to allow a person to put their thoughts and feelings into words. This is the area of the brain which is often affected by stroke patients. As a result of the fMRI's van der Kolk and their team were able to see from the scans that Broca's area went "offline" when a flashback was triggered.

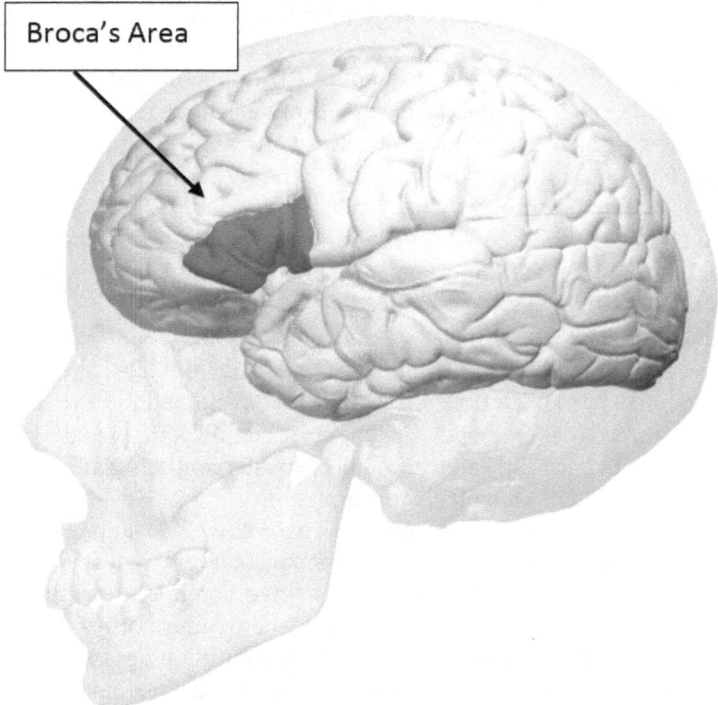

Figure 4.2 Broca's Area. *Source:* Database Center for Life Science, via Wikimedia Commons. Retrieved from https://commons.m.wikimedia.org/wiki/File:Broca%27s_ area_-_lateral_view.png#mw-jump-to-license

Another interesting finding of van der Kolk (2014) and his team was the way the right and left brain reacted during the fMRI. The scans indicated that images of past trauma activated the right hemisphere of the brain and deactivated the left side of the brain. It's important for us to recognize the "jobs" of the right and left brain so that we can truly understand what is happening to victims of trauma. As educators, this understanding will have a huge impact in the way we deliver instruction to our young victims.

Research regarding the left and right brain functionalities (known as the split-brain studies) began in the 1960s with Roger Sperry and Michael Gazzaniga (Gazzaniga, 2015). In their experiments, they presented stimuli to just one hemisphere or the other at a time and realized that the two halves of the brain acted independently, and each side had different processing styles.

As a result of their research and others that followed, many labeled the right brain as intuitive, emotional, visual, spatial, and tactual and left as linguistic, sequential, and analytical (van der Kolk, 2014). The left and right brain also remember past experiences in different ways as well. The right brain stores memories of sound, touch, smell, and the emotions they evoke. The left brain remembers facts, statistics, and vocabulary of events. Broca's area is found on the left side of the brain.

Therefore, "deactivation of the left hemisphere has a direct impact on the capacity to organize experiences into logical sequences and to translate our shifting feelings and perceptions into words" (van der Kolk, 2014, p. 45). The inability to sequence events causes difficulty in connecting cause-and-effect relationships. This can lead to difficulty in creating coherent plans for the future.

Being able to provide a complete narrative of a trauma event also may be difficult for the victim because of the way the brain has been impacted. Interestingly, trauma victims usually develop a "cover story" as a way of telling others the tragedy of what occurred. Their cover story can provide an explanation of their symptoms and behavior, but it is truly difficult to provide a coherent report of the experience with a beginning, middle, and end. This is why so many sexual assault victims are not always able to provide an exact account of their assault.

Receptive language is also impacted, as children may have difficulty understanding and processing information they are provided by others via speech. Comprehension is impaired, and as we know from the research, children need to be able to understand spoken language before they can express themselves (Craig, 2016). While Broca's area is related to the production of speech, another area, Wernicke's area is responsible for the comprehension of speech. Production of meaningful language can be impacted, and children may have difficulty with the written and spoken word.

As one might imagine, this can also create huge difficulties for children in the classroom as they try to learn new material every day. Executive functioning is lost as the left and right brain are impacted and not able synchronously communicate.

The following section will provide the strategies necessary to support children of trauma as they develop expressive and receptive language skills.

STRATEGIES TO SUPPORT LANGUAGE DEVELOPMENT

The following strategies can be used to support a child in the classroom who may be struggling with expressive and/or receptive language:

- Provide vocabulary lists for children to help them find the right words when speaking and writing.
- Offer pictures for students to support storytelling and sequencing of events to build expressive language skills.

- Tell students to focus on the directions you are about to give. This cues them in to be ready for the directions. Also, ask a student to summarize directions once you have given them, or have children work together in groups to summarize what they have heard.
- Encourage children to use graphic organizers to note ideas they are interested in writing or talking about. They can use pictures or words to record their ideas in the organizers. Using timelines also helps with expressive language and also teaches students to sequence events.
- Provide children with verbal prompts to solve problems and resolve conflicts with peers to support expressive language development.
- Teach children how to discuss an area of personal interest for 2–3 minutes.
- Teach children how to use self-talk to strengthen the sequential process of critical thinking.
- Using the Language Experience Approach (LEA), children can create a story of an event they all experienced. As each child provides a sentence, the teacher can write it on chart paper. This method supports expressive and receptive language and can offer other opportunities for teaching reading and writing skills.
- Implement dramatic play opportunities, and younger children will also benefit from the use of songs and fingerplays to support the development of expressive language skills. Children may need direct instruction on the use of some props because children of trauma may have limited experience. Providing a language-rich environment is imperative. (Sorrels, 2015)

IMPACT ON MEMORY

As educators, it's important for us to recognize there are different types of memory, each with an important job. Davis and Logie (1993) have recognized that memories are the organizational framework for children's development. For memorization to occur, all these different types of memory must work together effectively for a lasting memory to be implanted. We know that memories are imperative for providing history, understanding relationships, and learning from our mistakes and celebrating our accomplishments (Craig, 2008; Stevens et al., 2017). Therefore, we must be able to evaluate the distinct differences between long-term memory (which includes explicit and implicit memory) and short-term memory, as well as the subparts of these two sections of memory.

There are other significant functions that connect short- and long-term memory—such as recall and recognition—that are worth mentioning as well to have a full understanding of the parts making up our memory system. Research has provided us with information that proves memory is not a "unitary process," and stress or trauma seems to have different effects depending on the memory type (Luethi, Meier, & Sandi, 2009). Educators should be prepared to support students of trauma who have been affected and present memory struggles.

Short-Term Memory and Working Memory

Short-term memory is the ability to hold a small amount of information in an available state for a short period of time. Short-term memory allows temporary recall and the ability to remember and process information at the same time. Some have equated short-term memory and working memory as the same system, but in actuality, working memory is more of an entire theoretical framework for processing. Working memory uses temporary storage and manipulation of information, for which short-term memory is responsible (Baddeley & Hitch, 1974).

The hippocampus is the part of the brain that is responsible for the conversion from short-term to long-term memory. Trauma inhibits the hippocampus from transforming memories, and so at times these memories can remain in the short-term memory (Lindau et al., 2016). This is key to understanding how short-term memory is affected by trauma.

Long-Term Memory

Long-term memory is the storing station or a vast store of knowledge and a record of prior events (Cowan, 2008). There are two different types of long-term memory: (1) explicit memory and (2) implicit memory.

Explicit memory, sometimes referred to as declarative memory, is a conscious recall and a memory of facts or events. It is termed *explicit memory* because it consists of information that is explicitly stored and retrieved (Mastin, 2018). Explicit memory is used throughout the day as we recall or recollect events in the past. There are often two types of memory associated with explicit memory, semantic and episodic memory. Semantic memory is memory of general knowledge. Trauma can affect this part of the brain by preventing information from different parts of the brain from combining and making a semantic memory in long-term memory storage (National Institute for the Clinical Application of Behavioral Medicine, n.d.).

Episodic memory is more autobiographical memory of an event recalling the experience. For example, if you attended a wedding, you might remember who was there and who you sat with at the reception dinner table. Trauma can shut down episodic memory and fragment the sequence of events (National Institute for the Clinical Application of Behavioral Medicine, n.d.). The part of the brain responsible for creating and recalling episodic memory is the hippocampus (Eichenbaum, 2004; Stevens et al., 2017). Although many studies have explored the impact of the hippocampal structure as a result of traumatic stress, few have proven the impact stress has on the hippocampus.

Most recently, Stevens and colleagues (2017) and LeDoux and Muller (1997) found that in individuals exposed to trauma, re-experiencing symptoms do, in fact, impact the hippocampal structure. Furthermore, Samuelson (2011) reviewed literature demonstrating declarative memory deficits related to post-traumatic stress disorder in patients who suffered from political violence, childhood abuse, and rape.

Implicit memory, sometimes referred to as nondeclarative memory or unconscious memory, uses past experiences to remember things without thinking about them and is active prior to language acquisition (Craig, 2008; 2016). Many behaviors are on "auto-pilot," and implicit memory allows for this to occur. Examples of skills or habits formed as implicit memories could include riding a bike or swimming. Again, these memories are used automatically without even thinking of them.

The National Institute for the Clinical Application of Behavioral Medicine (www.nicabm.com) recognizes emotional and procedural memory as subsets of implicit memory. Emotional memory is the memory of the emotions you felt during an experience, and these emotions may be extremely painful if triggered after a trauma. The amygdala is the part of the brain that supports memory, especially during emotionally charged experiences (LeDoux & Muller, 1997; Stevens et al., 2017). Barbara Sorrels (2015) explains the way emotional memory is affected for a child of trauma: "If a child falls down on the playground, the sight of blood can trigger the memory of seeing someone get shot and the terror of the moment" (p. 44). Procedural memory is the memory of how to perform a common task without actively thinking, particularly the use of objects or maneuvering of body parts (Mastin, 2018). Trauma can affect procedural memory by changing the patterns of procedural memory. The striatum (part of the brain) is associated with producing procedural memory and creating new habits.

A person who has been affected by trauma may have a procedural memory or pattern of reaction that is activated in response to that particular stress or trauma. These body memories continue to cause extreme emotional and physical distress and do not allow a body to be at peace.

The following section will provide the strategies necessary to support children of trauma as they develop expressive and receptive language skills.

STRATEGIES TO SUPPORT LONG-TERM AND SHORT-TERM MEMORY

The following strategies can be used to support a child in the classroom who may be struggling with expressive and/or receptive language.

- Mnemonics: Using mnemonics can help make connections. A mnemonic is something we use to remember things easier. For example, using the acronym HOMES is a mnemonic to help us remember the Great Lakes (Huron, Ontario, Michigan, Erie, and Superior). Mnemonics can also be songs that help us to remember something as well. Mnemonic techniques use the visual cortex of the brain to simplify the complexity of memories. Simpler memories are more easily stored.
- Repetition: Reviewing concepts over and over aid in remembering information. In fact, an accommodation that is frequently used in Individualized Education Plans (IEPs) is repetition. Creating drills or games to help students remember information will aid in the retention of concepts.
- Concept maps: Concept maps are visual representations of information and are another strategy to bolster memory. They can include Venn Diagrams, graphic organizers, timelines, flowcharts, tables, and so on. Concept maps helps to chunk information and show links between concepts, making

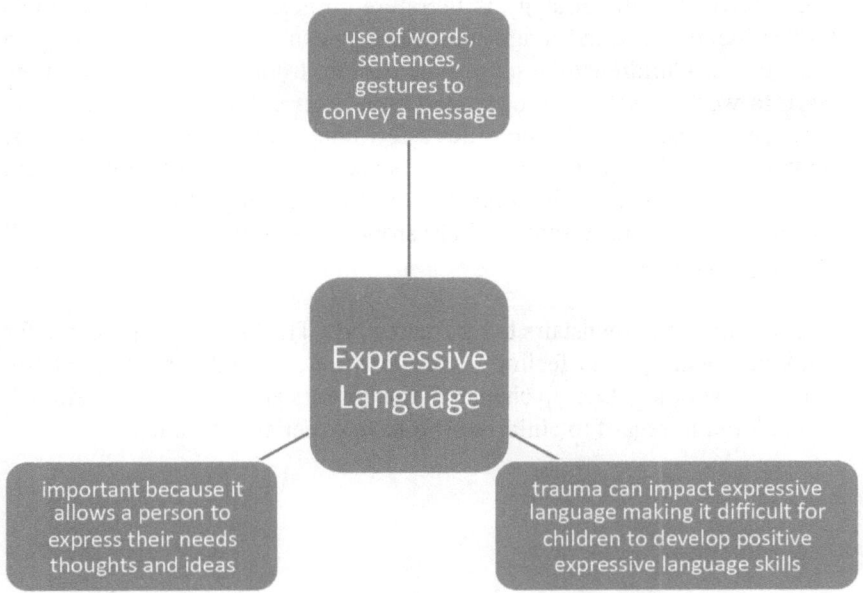

Figure 4.3 Expressive language concept map. *Source:* Colleen Lelli

it easier to remember information. Figure 4.1 (above) and figure 4.3 are examples of concept maps.
- Active reading strategies: Using active reading strategies will engage the learner and provide them the opportunity to comprehend the information they are reading. Questioning, connecting, and predicting are all reading strategies that will help students retain and comprehend the text they are reading. Question Answer Relationship (QAR) is another helpful reading-comprehension strategy. It encourages students to be active, strategic readers of texts. QAR outlines where information can be found: "In the Text" or "In my Head." It then breaks down the actual question-answer relationships into four types: Right There, Think and Search, Author and Me, and On My Own (Raphael, 1986). Underlining text, using sticky notes, and highlighting text are all important tools for active reading.
- Multisensory strategies: Using as many senses as possible will help students to process information and move that information into long-term memory. Many schools have adopted curricula that use a multisensory approach like the Wilson Reading System.
- Cooperative learning strategies: According to the seminal work by Slavin (1995), cooperative learning has been proven effective for all types of student learners. Peers can "teach" or review content, and it is a win-win for all students in the cooperative learning group. One example of a cooperative learning strategy is literature circles, which Harvey Daniels (1994) identified decades ago; this strategy has been used effectively in classrooms. Children of trauma will benefit from this strategy as they learn to work closely with peers and hone their expressive and receptive language skills. Table 4.1 provides a few cooperative learning strategies, how to use each strategy, and why it is useful. All of these strategies are useful because they build relational support among students, develop social skills, create a sense of classroom community, and support all learning styles.

- The upstairs and downstairs brain framework: The brain is responsible for thinking, memory, and feelings, and there are different parts of the brain that must work together. In chapter 5, the upstairs and downstairs brain will be explored in regard to children who have experienced trauma.

Table 4.1. Cooperative Learning Strategies

Name of Strategy	How to Use the Strategy	Why the Strategy Is Useful
Think Ink Pair Share	A question is posed to the students by the teacher. The students have time to think about the response and can write a response and/or draw a response. They then pair up with a partner to share their responses.	This is a quick, easy strategy that can be implemented in almost any lesson. All students have the opportunity to use both expressive and receptive skills, and it strengthens short-term memory while students are learning new information and connecting it with prior knowledge.
Jigsaw	Students are placed in home groups. While in home groups, students are provided a task, and each take on an "expert" role to learn the assigned material. After students meet in their expert groups, the home groups are reconvened to share what they learned.	Students engage with one another in small groups. Every student has a "job" to complete or role to play, so it truly is the epitome of a cooperative learning strategy.
Inside Outside Circle	Students stand in two concentric circles, with the same number of students in each circle. The inside circle and outside circles face each other. The inside circle shares or asks questions of their partner in the outside circle. The teacher's role is to prompt them to then switch roles and/or turn the circles to have a new partner.	The benefit of the inside outside circle is the opportunity for students to use material they have written or learned to share with a partner.
Showdown	Task cards with various questions are place face-down between a group of 4–5 students. A chosen leader asks the question to the other group members. The members write down their response on paper or a small whiteboard. The leader announces, "Showdown," and all members show their answers at once. Teams can also keep score. Leaders rotate throughout the group. An alternative can also be to have students pair together and develop their responses as a paired team.	As a formative assessment and cooperative learning technique, this is an opportunity for students to work collaboratively on something they have learned. It is useful for all students to develop their expressive language skills, and it reinforces information processing of new content.

Adapted from Bennett (2016) and POPFASD (n.d.).

REFERENCES

Baddeley, A. D., & Hitch, G. J. (1974). Working memory. In G. H. Bower (Ed.), *The psychology of learning and motivation* (vol. 8). Academic Press.

Bennett, M. (2016). *Examples of cooperative learning strategies.* KNILT. https://tccl.arcc.albany.edu/knilt/index.php/Examples_of_Cooperative_Learning_Strategies

Cowan, N. (2008). What are the differences between long-term, short-term, and working memory? *Progress in Brain Research, 169,* 323–338.

Craig, S. (2008). *Reaching and teaching children who hurt: Strategies for your classroom.* Paul H. Brookes Publishing Company.

Craig, S. (2016). *Trauma-sensitive schools: Learning communities transforming children's lives, K–5.* Teachers College Press.

Daniels, H. (1994). *Literature circles: Voice and choice in the student-centered classroom.* Stenhouse.

Davis, G. M., & Logie, R. I. (Eds.) (1993). *Memory in everyday life.* Elsevier.

Donegan, N. S. (2003). Amygdala hyperreactivity in borderline personality disorder: Implications for emotional dysregulation. *Biological Psychiatry, 54*(11), 1284–1293.

Eichenbaum, H. (2004). Hippocampus: Cognitive processes and neural representations that underlie declarative memory. *Neuron, 44*(1), 109–120.

Gazzaniga, M. S. (2015). *Tales from both sides of the brain: A life in neuroscience.* HarperCollins.

Ledoux, J. E., & Muller, J. (1997). Emotional memory and psychopathology. *Philosophical transactions of the Royal Society of London. Series B, Biological Sciences, 352*(1362), 1719–1726.

Lindau, M., Almkvist, O., & Mohammed, A. H. (2016). Effects of stress on learning and memory. In G. Fink (Ed.), *Stress: Concepts, cognition, emotion, and behavior* (pp. 153–160). Elsevier.

Luethi, M., Meier, B., & Sandi, C. (2009). Stress effects on working memory, explicit memory, and implicit memory for neutral and emotional stimuli in healthy men. *Frontiers in Behavioral Neuroscience, 2*(5), 1–9.

Mastin, L. (2018). *Declarative (explicit) & procedural (implicit) memory.* http://www.human-memory.net/types_declarative.html

Minzenberg, M. F. (2008). Front limbic structural changes in borderline personality disorder. *Journal of Psychiatric Research, 42*(9), 727–733.

National Institute for the Clinical Application of Behavioral Medicine. (n.d.). *How trauma can impact four types of memory.* https://www.nicabm.com/trauma-how-trauma-can-impact-4-types-of-memory-infographic

POPFASD. (n.d.). *Cooperative learning techniques.* https://static.fasdoutreach.ca/www/toolbox/c/Cooperative_Learning_Techniques.pdf

Raphael, T. E. (1986). Teaching question-answer relationships. *The Reading Teacher, 39,* 516–520.

Samuelson, K. W. (2011). Post-traumatic stress disorder and declarative memory functioning: A review. *Dialogues in Clinical Neuroscience, 13*(3), 346–351.

Slavin, R. E. (1995). *Cooperative learning: Theory, research, and practice* (2nd edition). Allyn & Bacon.

Sorrels, B. (2015). *Reaching and teaching children exposed to trauma*. Gryphon House.

Stevens, J. S., Reddy, R., Kim, Y. J., van Rooij, S. J. H., Ely, T. D., Hamann, S., Ressler, K. J., & Jovanovic, T. (2017). Episodic memory after trauma exposure: Medial temporal lobe function is positively related to re-experiencing and inversely related to negative affect symptoms. *Neuroimage Clinical, 17*, 650–658. https://doi:10.1016/j.nicl.2017.11.016

Sylvestre, A., Bussières, È.-L., & Bouchard, C. (2015). Language problems among abused and neglected children: A meta-analytic review. *Child Maltreatment, 21*(1), 47–58. https://doi.org/10.1177/1077559515616703

van der Kolk, B. A. (2014). *The body keeps the score: Brain, mind and body in the healing of trauma*. Penguin Books.

Yehuda, N. (2005). The language of dissociation. *Journal of Trauma & Dissociation, 6*(1), 10–29.

5

Impact of Trauma on Relationships and Self-Regulation

> This chapter will provide:
> - an analysis of the three categories used to explain infant and toddler attachment styles: secure, insecure avoidant, and insecure ambivalent/resistant;
> - a discussion of how trauma can affect healthy attachment and lead to further difficulty in various relationships, including teacher-student relationships;
> - information about the stress response system and how to use this system in a positive manner to self-regulate feelings and behaviors;
> - the importance of the upstairs and downstairs brain in self-regulation of behaviors and feelings; and
> - strategies to support developing positive relationships and positive self-regulation skills.

RELATIONSHIPS AND ATTACHMENT THEORY

Attachment patterns are devised as a result of a child's early experiences with caregivers; they develop over time as the attachment patterns are internalized and shape how the individual views themselves and the connections they have with others in close relationships. This is related very closely to Erik Erikson's (1963) theory and his first stage of development known as trust versus mistrust, discussed in chapter 3. John Bowlby (1969) brought together different perspectives from psychoanalytic theory, learning theory, and cognitive theory to describe attachment theory.

In attachment theory, Bowlby tries to explain how and why children form bonds with their parents (he primarily focused on mothers, at the time) and caregivers (van der Horst & van der Veer, 2010). He further describes attachment as "an intense and enduring emotional bond that is rooted in the function and protection of infants from danger" (Palm, 2014). Biologically, attachment behaviors are used to guarantee survival. Infants use their signaling capabilities to communicate and also to initiate social engagement by using cooing and smiling (Palm, 2014; van der Horst & van der Veer, 2010). This provides a safe place for children to explore and to come back to in times of uncertainty.

Part of John Bowlby's research was defining a concept he called internal working models, a construct that he believed forms the basis of personality (Bowlby, 1973). Infants develop expectations about their role in attracting attention from caregivers or their incapability of not being able to gain needed attention. They also learn others' roles in relationships. For instance, they learn who they can trust, who they can readily access, and the responsiveness of their caregivers.

They also will notice if a caregiver is not trustworthy or is inaccessible and unresponsive. "The development of this internal working model is so relationship-bound that the child internalizes both sides of the experienced attachment relationship and learns caregiving while receiving care" (Alexander, 1992, p. 186). Children are captivated by faces and voices and sensitive to facial expressions, tone of voice, and posture (van der Kolk, 2014). In other words, children learn what to expect from others and how to interact with others (Jennings, 2019).

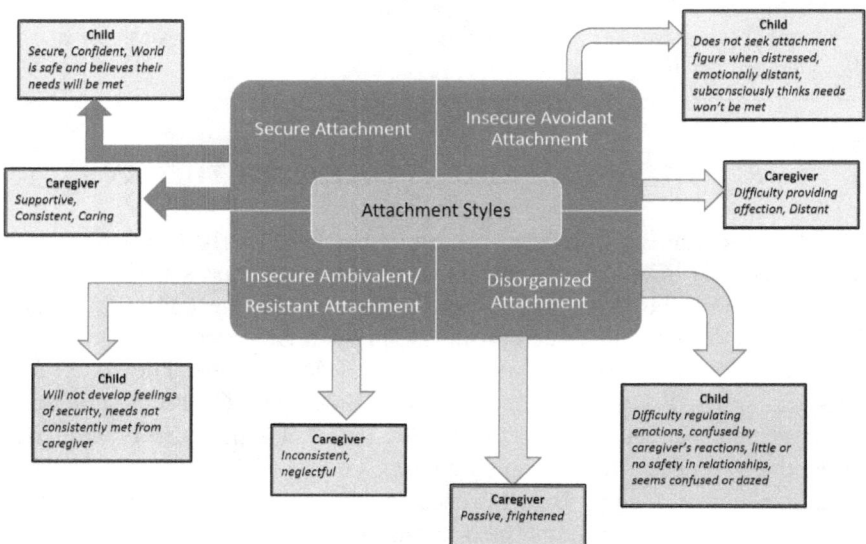

Figure 5.1 Attachment styles. *Source:* Colleen Lelli

Ainsworth and Bell (1970) furthered Bowlby's research with her seminal study titled "Stranger Situation." She discovered that mother-child interactions in the first 3 months predicted 12-month-olds' behavior in a laboratory setting. Ainsworth and her team observed toddlers' behaviors in a series of eight brief separation episodes in a room with toys. They observed the child's reactions upon the entrance and leaving of a stranger and of the child's mother. The specific reactions they observed were the emotional and behavioral responses to separating from a primary caregiver and then reuniting with that caregiver. Ainsworth and her team noticed how the child adjusted, or not, and noted that the behaviors signified a particular relational pattern. As a result of the study, Ainsworth and Bell (1970) identified three categories to explain infant and toddler attachment styles: secure, insecure avoidant, and insecure ambivalent/resistant.

Secure Attachment

Babies and children who are securely attached will feel confident that their needs are being met by the attachment figure. More specifically, a child's need for safety, comfort, security, and emotional care are keys to developing attachment. The caregiver will be utilized during times of distress, but other times the child is confident to explore their environment knowing the caregiver is available if needed. As secure attachment develops, an important piece of this development is emotional attunement. Attunement "starts at the most subtle physical level of interaction between babies and their caretakers and babies feel that their needs are being met and understood," (van der Kolk, 2014).

Securely attached children will learn to differentiate between situations they can control and situations where they need help. They acquire a sense of agency and recognize that their actions can change how they feel and how others respond (van der Kolk, 2014). Both children and adults find great ease in interacting with securely attached children because they are able to engage in relationships with support and empathy.

A child with a secure attachment will learn that the world is a safe place with people in their lives who are caring, supportive, and a safe haven (Jennings, 2019). Children learn that other people have feelings and thoughts, and they develop self-awareness, empathy, impulse control, and self-motivation. Furthermore, this will guide how individuals identify and cope with stress throughout their lifetime (Ogle et al., 2015). In fact, a secure attachment relationship with a caregiver is the strongest predictor of resilience after disclosure of abuse (in this sense, ease in adjustment over time and fewer trauma symptoms). This is a perfect example of how when a child is faced with small or significant stressors, the attachment can be a great source of strength.

As noted by Ainsworth and Bell's (1970) seminal research study, a securely attached child will explore the room freely when the caregiver is present and may be distressed when the caregiver leaves. The child may explore the room and toys less when the caregiver is not present but will be happy upon return of the caregiver. The child may cry and approach the caregiver to be comforted and held. At the very least, the child will at least greet the caregiver. Once comforted, the child will independently explore the room. Because of the responsiveness of the caregiver, the child knows they are able to depend on their caregiver during times of need or while under stress.

Insecure Avoidant

Unlike the child in a secure attachment relationship with their caregiver, a child who is considered insecure avoidant will not seek their attachment figure when distressed. It appears as if the child is not bothered at all by the mother leaving, almost as if the child does not notice the separation. Instead, the child may be affected by the separation physically, with their heart rate increasing, being in a state of hyperarousal. This pattern was described by van der Kolk (2014) as "dealing but not feeling."

The body is dealing with the separation, but there is no related emotional expression. This is most likely because the caregiver is not meeting their needs through their insensitive nature and/or rejecting their needs. The caregivers may have difficulty snuggling and holding the child. They are unavailable during times of emotional distress when the child needs them most. Facial expressions and voices are not used to create a pleasurable back-and-forth interaction with the infant or toddler. Craig (2016) identifies this as "serve and return" interactions.

An avoidant-insecure child will not explore much and will not show much emotion when the caregiver leaves. Preference for the caregiver over a stranger is not prevalent. Upon return of the caregiver, the child may avoid or ignore the caregiver all together. Furthermore, as noted in the "Stranger Situation" research, children may even display episodes of aggression toward the caregiver within the home setting (Ainsworth & Bell, 1970; Ainsworth et al., 1978).

Once these children reach school age, teachers may notice that the child acts ambivalent or as if they don't care. In actuality this child is hurt, sad, and/or angry. Aggressive behaviors may be noted as the child tries to protect herself against further rejection from classmates (Jennings, 2019).

Insecure Ambivalent/Resistant

An infant or toddler who is insecure ambivalent/resistant will not develop feelings of security from the caregiver. Children will cry, yell, cling, or scream. Van der Kolk (2014) notes this as "feeling but not dealing." The child is unable to deal with the lack of attunement in their direct environment, and they are only left with their overwhelming emotional response. Children will be difficult to soothe, and interaction provided from the attachment figure will not result in feelings of comfort even though they are in extreme distress when their caregivers are not present. Their needs are not consistently met from the primary caregiver.

During the Ainsworth and Bell (1970) study, the insecure-resistant child was like the avoidant child in that they didn't explore much on their own. The insecure-resistant child was upset when the caregiver left and was guarded in front of strangers. When the caregiver returned, although the child wanted to be close to the caregiver, he/she was very angry with the caregiver for leaving them behind, and therefore, the child may have rejected the caregiver's attempt at contact (Ainsworth et al., 1978).

As these children progress into school age, they may anger easily or be frustrated, anxious, and impulsive. They may have low self-esteem, which can cause victimization or bullying (Jennings, 2019). These children will seek attention whether it is positive or negative and at times cause conflict to receive any type of response from the teacher. Other behaviors that may be noticeable include older children being nervous about what others may do or think about them in a negative sense—for example, "They don't like me." Some children may not have many friendships and will try to monopolize a single friendship by telling the friend not to be friends with others.

As educators, recognizing attachment theory and the various categories associated with infant and toddler attachment styles is necessary for us to provide the best educational strategies in the classroom. Furthermore, it may also offer means of better understanding the complex behaviors some children demonstrate in school.

Potentially, this could offer a sense of relief for educators, as it decreases confusion and frustration and increases empathy and confidence in moving forward. We also need to understand how trauma can cause attachment to be detrimental for a child and their future well-being.

Caregiving Styles and Culture

It's important to note that parenting styles are driven at times by historical or cultural practices. Being an attuned caregiver can appear very different in one family versus another. It's important as educators that we are culturally responsive and have a firm knowledge base of the cultures of the children in our classroom.

Also, caregiving is challenging in a number of ways, but for secure attachment to be developed, a caregiver needs to be consistently attuned to the child and to regularly provide security and care. The caregiving style does not have to be perfect but should be consistent. This means caregivers who work full-time outside the home or have partial custody and/or have life challenges that are faced on a daily basis, all are able to have securely attached relationships with their children as long as the parenting style is consistent in providing security and care.

HOW TRAUMA AFFECTS ATTACHMENT

Attachment theory provides for us an explanation of healthy relationships with children and their caregivers and provides a foundation for all further development. We've learned that infants will develop an "organized strategy to deal with the strains and stresses of separations, strange environments, illness, and other stressful or threatening events" (Bakermans-Kranenburg et al., 2005). When a child does not feel safe and if their environment is unpredictable or they are victimized by their caregiver, this will cause confusion and mistrust regarding the world around them. Their needs will be unmet, and a disorganized attachment may prevail, leading to impairment of future relationships.

Disorganized Attachment

A disorganized attachment can form when a child may experience negative physical or emotional behaviors from their caregiver or behavior that can be seen as life threatening. The child is faced with a dilemma—how do they seek safety when the very person who is supposed to keep them safe is causing them immense harm? Children are born with an instinct to seek care from the adults who care for them. Once a child realizes that support is not being provided and they are not safe, a child may block what is happening to them from their consciousness. A parent's unpredictable behavior can lead to a lack of an organized strategy for meeting the child's needs, and as a result, the child will not feel safe. They detach from the situation around them, and thus a disorganized attachment is formed with the caregiver.

In the "Stranger Situation" procedure Mary Ainsworth conducted, it was noted that children with disorganized attachment conveyed odd or hesitant behaviors (Main & Solomon, 1986). For example, some children ran up to the parent but then pulled away or ran away from the parent. Some hit the parent, and others demonstrated varying emotional responses during the Stranger Situation procedure. A child wants to first seek comfort from the parent as their immediate instinct may inform them but then ultimately become more fearful as their disorganized symptoms are activated.

Parents or caregivers could unintentionally cause a disorganized attachment with the child. A parent's own unresolved trauma or loss they previously experienced could unintentionally scare or provide an unhealthy relationship with the child. Research has also shown that trauma involving caregivers may significantly disrupt caregiver-child attachment, leading to insecure or disorganized attachment (Main & Goldwyn, 1984; Ainsworth & Bell, 1970; Bowlby, 1969; van der Kolk, 2014; Ogle et al., 2015).

Main and Goldwyn (1984) developed a tool named the Adult Attachment Interview and found that any unresolved trauma such as abuse or neglect in a caregiver's life is the best predictor of disorganized attachment between a caregiver and a child. Unfortunately, disorganized attachment can be passed from generation to generation.

Caregivers with unresolved trauma may have difficulty with the range of emotions a child exhibits, and the caregivers will react to their children with fear or other emotions that are not appropriate or helpful during the child's moment of need. During these moments, the caregivers may not even recognize that they are responding inappropriately. They may act in ways that don't make sense, and this sets up an unpredictable relationship with their child. The child will not know how to react, causing confusion in the moment and a confusing relational pattern for children over time.

A child with a disorganized attachment will find it challenging to self-soothe and/or regulate their emotions (Bakermans-Kranenburg et al., 2005; Ainsworth & Bell, 1970). They may struggle socially and have difficulty forming friendships and trusting others. They will have difficulty managing stress and may even demonstrate hostile or aggressive behaviors. They view their world as precarious and chaotic.

Reading social cues and interacting with others leads to success in school and in other environments, and a child with a disorganized attachment style may have significant challenges in school both socially and academically. Many of the behaviors mentioned here that educators may see in the classroom could be a result of children living with current or past trauma and/or not having a secure attachment.

Healing from a disorganized attachment is possible. Bakermans-Kranenburg and colleagues (2005) note that sensitivity-focused interventions can prevent or change attachment disorganization. One tool that has been found to be helpful later in life is the creation of a narrative to aid in the healing process.

The narrative helps people understand how earlier experiences are still affecting them. Once they are able to do this, they can discover healthier strategies to process their unresolved trauma. This will allow them to engage in healthy, productive, secure relationships and lead to resilience of the mind.

THE TEACHER-STUDENT RELATIONSHIP

Attachment theory has been used to guide and inspire teacher-child relationships. Can teacher-child relationships be considered an attachment relationship? There are several similarities that suggest the teacher-child relationship serves in this attachment capacity; however, there have been questions raised as well that suggest it may not necessarily fit the attachment theory suggested by Bowlby and Ainsworth.

Research has proven that any consistent, supportive adult is a greatest source of resilience for children (Jennings, 2019; Burke-Harris, 2018; Ginsburg & Jablow, 2006). Additional research has proven that a relationship with a caring, nurturing teacher can support students in the classroom but more importantly is significantly helpful for students with multiple risk factors (Sabol & Pianta, 2012; Hughes, 2012). Teachers are with children more than any other adults (outside caregivers) and serve as role models for healthy social and emotional behavior. Teachers are uniquely positioned to offer the safety, care, and security needed by children while promoting healthy relationships and the motivation to learn.

The differences regarding relationships between children and parents/caregivers and children and teachers has been researched for some time. Parents will have an emotional investment in their children—much more so than teachers will possess. Additionally, while teachers do engage in caregiving behaviors, these are generally more restricted than parents, as the teacher's primary role is instructional (Verschueren & Koomen, 2012). A parent or caregiver's role is more indirect and broad and includes teaching of values and morals (Verschueren & Koomen, 2012).

Children in most school systems change teachers every year, and an exclusive, durable bond may not form as it does with parents. Furthermore, in middle and secondary schools, students will interact with multiple teachers throughout the day (Verschueren & Koomen, 2012). Verschueren and Koomen (2012) contend that teachers could be regarded as "ad hoc attachment figures" but they do recognize that "the role of the teacher as an attachment figure is expected to be of greater importance" (p. 207). They further go on to state that because of the child's lack of self-regulation, help provided by the teacher will be a significant support for survival and growth (Verschueren & Koomen, 2012).

In the field of education, the affective quality of teacher-child relationships was not studied frequently in the past. Most recently the relationship dimensions of closeness, conflict, and dependency have been assessed using the Student-Teacher Relationship Scale (STRS) (Pianta, 2001) which was developed based on behaviors derived from attachment theory to assess teacher-child relationship quality from the perspective of the teacher.

Using the STRS, the dimension of closeness investigates the degree to which the child found value in using the teacher as a safe haven while viewing the relationship as open and warm, which is associated with positive academic and behavioral outcomes. The concept of conflict refers to the "expressions of negative emotion and lack of rapport between the teacher and the student and is associated with poor academic and behavioral outcomes" (Jennings, 2019).

Dependency refers to the way a student will cling to the teacher. Jennings (2019) mentions that dependency has been associated with attachment disorders, and teachers need to be aware and sensitive when planning and connecting with students in meaningful learning activities. Moreover, on the STRS, if a teacher rates dependency as high, this indicates their perception that the child fails to use the teacher as a secure base from which to explore (Verschueren & Koomen, 2012).

Further research based on attachment theory asserts that children "internalize experiences with their primary attachment figures and tend to carry these internalized models or relational schemata forward to the new relationships they form" (Verschueren & Koomen, 2012). For instance, the question regarding whether mother-child attachment security leads to relationship continuity between the student and teacher and to internalizing and externalizing problems in late childhood was explored by O'Connor and colleagues (2012).

Other studies revealed that children with secure maternal attachment histories were more likely to establish close and supportive relationships with first-grade teachers (Verschueren et al., 2012). This then led positively to children perceiving competency in social activities and positive peer relationships. In other words, children internalize the secure attachment with their caregiver and then are able to "leverage" those relational tools in future relationships, such as with teachers and their peers.

Children who have the opportunity to form positive relationships with adults will learn through these consistent relationships how to regulate their emotions and internal states. Teachers can use their own affective competence to support children as they gain control of their behavior and emotions (Craig, 2008). Students will learn appropriate decision-making and self-management skills through quality instruction in the classroom. Children learning appropriate language skills will also be able to monitor their behavior with instruction and encouragement from their teacher.

Hughes (2012) contends that "we know enough" to apply the results of the research studies focusing on attachment security between teachers and students. We know that increasing teachers' abilities to provide positive social and emotional learning environments will result in improving students' learning and behavior in the classroom. Teachers who are highly sensitive will make positive gains with children with less secure relationships (Buyse et al., 2011).

If a teacher is insensitive in the early years of a child's education, research has shown that the child will more likely continue to have difficult relationships with future teachers. By understanding attachment theory, educators can create and maintain positive relationships with their students. As a result, positive gains will be seen in students' behaviors, teacher-student relationships, and peer relationships as well.

SELF-REGULATION AND STRESS RESPONSE SYSTEM

We now understand the importance of a primary attachment figure for a child and the long-lasting developmental support that they can provide. For a child to learn self-regulation skills, a secure caregiver is necessary. Self-regulation is the ability to "regulate emotions in a socially appropriate matter" (Craig, 2008, p. 98). Emotional regulation involves both cognitive and psychological processes, control of bodily functions, managing emotions, maintaining focus and attention, and lastly, making considerate decisions (Peterson, 2014).

As Craig (2008) explains, children cognitively need to be able to know how they are feeling and then be able to find the vocabulary to express those emotions. Psychologically, children need to control how they're feeling and control how those feelings affect their internal being.

Stress regulation will develop through maturation. A positive caregiver will provide the child with an appropriate model for positive interactions and examples of how the child can monitor their own behavior. "Our ability to regulate ourselves in the face of stress is rooted in how well we were regulated in the first three years of life" (Sorrels, 2015, p. 101). A primary attachment figure can provide comfort and encouragement for a child to self-monitor and adjust their own behavior (Craig, 2008). Children who trust their caregivers are able to explore their full range of emotions (Wiebler, 2013).

An environment built on consistency, predictability, and structure leads the child to know that the primary caregiver will still be there for them and love them. Skills in perspective taking, or understanding what others think and feel, are also developed while the caregivers model the appropriate behavior and directly instruct these skills (Peterson, 2014).

We learned in chapter 1 the effects the stress-response system can have on a person's body. If the stress-response system is constantly being run over and over again, the brain will have difficulty processing, and this leads to a host of difficulties, including self-regulation.

A child who has suffered trauma or complex traumas will feel as though they are in a constant state of hyperarousal. Because of this constant state of hyperarousal, they perceive they are in danger at all times. Furthermore, they have feelings of fear, rage, and shame as mental images rooted within themselves (Craig, 2008).

As a result of these feelings and hyperaroused state, a child may feel both out of control and uncared for if they have a caregiver not providing the emotional stability that is necessary to overcome significant traumas. Educators will witness internalized and externalized behaviors because of a child's inability to self-regulate emotions. Table 5.1 lists possible internalized and externalized behaviors that a child may exhibit.

A child who is exhibiting difficult behaviors in the classroom is not regulated, and their nervous system is in overdrive as they experience stressful situations. A child who is acting out is doing so to "regulate" the overwhelming sensations they are feeling at that moment. They need the help of an adult to move back to a state of peace (Forbes, 2012). The "fight, flight, or freeze" system is in overdrive. Another way to understand the way students respond to stressful situations and the response of the nervous system is to understand the upstairs and downstairs brain.

Table 5.1. Examples of Internalized and Externalized Behaviors

Internalized behaviors are behaviors that result from negativity focused inward.

Blaming themselves/ oversensitivity	Feelings of loneliness and guilt	Sadness
Social withdrawal	Anxiety	Fearfulness
Sleeping problems	Persistent worrying	Complaints of illness (headache, stomachache)

Externalized behaviors are problem behaviors that are directed toward the external environment.

Fighting	Cursing	Stealing
Temper tantrums	Impulsive behaviors	Destruction of property
Arson	Noncompliant behaviors	Negative reactions to sharing and taking turns
Lying	Being reactive	Aggressive behavior
Inconsolable crying		

THE UPSTAIRS AND DOWNSTAIRS BRAIN

We have learned from neuroscience research the ways sensory input enters the brain. It will enter the lower parts of the brain first and then will proceed to the higher, more complex parts of the brain. If the incoming information is connected with a previous threat, the stress response system is activated prior to the prefrontal cortex, or the thinking part of the brain can interpret and then process the information (Perry & Szalavitz, 2006; Craig, 2008). This is how triggers occur. A trigger is an unconscious connection that evokes extreme reaction to a memory of a trauma. The response is so intense that the higher complex areas of the brain are not activated in time for a healthy mediation.

Another way to consider the brain's operations is the work done by Dr. Dan Siegel and Dr. Tina Payne Bryson (2011), in which they explain that the brain is similar to a house and can be divided into the upstairs and downstairs brain. The downstairs brain, which would be the lower part of the brain, includes the brain stem and limbic system.

These lower areas are responsible for such functions as (1) breathing and blinking, (2) other innate functions including the fight-and-flight system, and (3) strong emotions. Strong emotions (like anger and fear) as well as bodily functions and instincts all live in the downstairs brain (Siegel & Bryson, 2011). The metaphor of a house is used because in a house all of the family's basic needs are generally met in the downstairs areas—the kitchen, dining room, bathroom, and so on.

The upstairs brain, on the other hand, consists of the cerebral cortex, where more "intricate mental processes take place like thinking, imagining, and planning" (Siegel & Bryson, 2011, p. 40). Higher-order thinking and analytical thinking occurs here. When an upstairs brain works well, a person can take in the emotions from the downstairs brain, regulate those emotions, and consider consequences before responding.

Some of the characteristics of an upstairs brain include sound decision making and planning, control over emotions and body, self-understanding, empathy, and morality. Of course, this means there needs to be an integration of the downstairs and upstairs brain, and therefore the staircase between the two is extremely important. The upstairs brain can help to modulate the strong emotions that may creep up as a result of stressful or trying situations. Likewise, the downstairs brain is important because we don't want to base all of our decisions off of the upstairs brain because emotions are needed for making decisions throughout life.

A parent's role is extremely important in guiding children to use this staircase as they regulate their emotions and learn to make decisions of their own. A nurturing caregiver can ensure they are modeling and explaining the importance of our upstairs and downstairs brain to help us to problem-solve as we regulate our emotions. Developmentally, it is essential that caregivers consider the child's needs and capabilities before expecting an upstairs brain that makes all the "right" decisions. It's important to note that the upstairs brain is not fully developed until the mid-20s (Siegel & Bryson, 2011).

This means that the parts of the brain responsible for empathy, positive decision making, self-understanding, and control of emotions are still in construction mode, and children in the best of circumstances will have difficulty at times using that part of the brain. As Siegel and Bryson (2011) note, children or young adults will be "trapped downstairs" without the use of the upstairs. Because of this "entrapment," children may fly off the handle or flip their lid.

In the case of a child with a trauma history being triggered by their environment, the child will "flip their lid," as they are unable to use their upstairs brain because their downstairs brain or the amygdala part of the brain has taken over. They are for the moment not able to control their body and emotions because they cannot access their upstairs brain, which includes higher-order thinking, solving problems, and considering others' feelings. The child has flipped their lid—they are unable to use their entire brain (Siegel & Bryson, 2011).

As educators, understanding attachment theory and how the brain works (and in simplest terms in this case, the upstairs and downstairs brain) provides us with opportunities to support a child's cognitive and emotional development.

Strategies to Support Developing Relationships

- Cooperative learning (Johnson & Johnson, 2009) involves a group of two to six heterogeneously grouped students working together toward a common goal as they share ideas and help each other with answers to questions and divide job duties. For a long time, cooperative learning has been considered a beneficial pedagogical tool to use in the classroom to support all learners. While children of trauma are no different than typical students, there are a few tips to engage students of trauma who may generally struggle with expressive language and self-regulation. Wiebler (2013) suggests that we place students living with trauma, chronic stress, and/or violence with partners who already have strong empathy and social skills. Johnson and Johnson (2009) further assert that deliberately assigning students to pairs or small groups and giving them a specific role will be helpful. Mini-lessons provided by the teacher to model and teach effective listening skills is also imperative.

- Craig (2008) recommends team-building exercises to provide children the opportunity to connect with one another. Discussing afterward how it felt to rely on one another will help to build relationships and class community.
- Support children to learn that disruptions in relationships can be repaired (Craig, 2008). When an aggressive behavior occurs, teach students how to talk out the problem, and encourage them to make amends with the student they were aggressive toward.
- Actively teach students to see things from another perspective. There are many ways this can be accomplished. One way is to read children's literature and have students retell the story from another character's perspective. There are also many familiar childhood tales that tell the story from another perspective—for example, telling the story of the "Three Little Pigs" from the wolf's perspective (Marlowe & Hayden, 2013).
- There are lots of little ways to develop relationships with students in your classroom: greeting them each day at the door with a special handshake, sharing appropriate information about yourself with the child and finding something in common, having sharing days where positive attributes about each other are shared, going to an extracurricular activity a child is participating in, and telling a child how much they were missed when they were not in school for a day. Another great idea is at the start of each day, have four blank sticky notes on your desk. By the end of the day, make sure you give those notes to four different students providing a special message of encouragement. Sometimes a child just needs to know someone is there for them and willing to support them—even when their behavior is pushing you away.

Strategies to Support Developing Self-Regulation

- Using the Positive Behavioral Intervention and Supports (PBIS) framework is a way for schools to encourage good behavior and teach children about their own behavior. The focus here is prevention, not punishment. PBIS informs children of the behavior expectations and teaches those behaviors throughout the school day, similar to how any other subject is taught.
- Provide a visual daily schedule in the classroom and/or for the child's desk. The schedule should be as consistent as possible every day. Any activity that is out of the ordinary (e.g., fire drill, assembly, etc.) should be reviewed at the start of each day.
- Provide safe opportunities to explore human emotions through role plays, drama, and literature (Craig, 2008).
- Over the years, I've been surprised at the number of classrooms I've entered that did not have the classroom rules prominently displayed. As

Marlowe and Hayden (2013) note there are three main reasons for establishing rules: (1) safety, (2) consistency, and (3) caring. Interestingly, these reasons closely align to what is needed for a positive attachment relationship! Children of trauma may not have experienced consistency in their life from adults. Inconsistency can lead to anxiety and mistrust. Children of trauma may also not have experienced healthy, consistent, and caring relationships from adults. Classroom rules can be simple and also change as the year goes on. As Marlowe and Hayden (2013) note, a teacher may choose to have two sets of rules: one that the teacher has developed and a second that the class developed. Always make the rules positive, clear, and simple.

- Planning and goal setting are strategies that can be used in the classroom to support self-regulation. Short-term goals can be used to attain longer-term goals. Planning can help students develop goals and strategies to be successful. Three stages can be followed for planning: (1) setting a goal for a learning task; (2) establishing strategies needed to achieve that goal; and (3) determining the time and resources needed to reach that goal (Schunk, 2001).

REFERENCES

Ainsworth, M. D. S., & Bell, S. M. (1970). Attachment, exploration, and separation: Illustrated by the behavior of one-year-olds in a strange situation. *Child Development, 41*, 49–67.

Ainsworth, M. D. S., Blehar, M. C., Waters, E., & Wall, S. (1978). *Patterns of attachment: A psychological study of the strange situation*. Erlbaum.

Alexander, P. C. (1992). Application of attachment theory to the study of sexual abuse. *Journal of Consulting and Clinical Psychology, 60*(2), 185–195.

Bakermans-Kranenburg, M. J., van Ijzendoorn, M. H., & Juffer, F. (2005). Disorganized infant attachment and preventive interventions: A review and meta-analysis. *Infant Mental Health Journal, 26*, 191–216.

Bowlby, J. (1969). *Attachment and loss, volume 1: Attachment*. Basic Books.

Bowlby, J. (1973). *Attachment and loss, volume 2: Separation*. Basic Books.

Burke-Harris, N. (2018). *The deepest well: Healing the long-term effects of childhood adversity*. Bluebird Publishing.

Buyse, E., Verschueren, K., & Doumen, S. (2011). Preschoolers' attachment to mother and risk for adjustment problems in kindergarten: Can teachers make a difference? *Social Development, 20*, 33–50.

Craig, S. (2008). *Reaching and teaching children who hurt: Strategies for your classroom*. Paul H. Brookes Publishing Company.

Craig, S. (2016). *Trauma-sensitive schools: Learning communities transforming children's lives, K–5*. Teachers College Press.

Erikson, E. H. (1963). *Childhood and society.* Norton.
Forbes, H. T. (2012). *Help for Billy: A beyond consequences approach to helping challenging children in the classroom.* Beyond Consequences Institute LLC.
Ginsburg, K. R., & Jablow, M. M. (2006). *Building resilience in children and teens: Giving kids roots and wings.* American Academy of Pediatrics.
Hughes, J. N. (2012). Teacher-student relationships and school adjustment: Progress and remaining challenges. *Attachment and Human Development, 14*(3), 319–327.
Jennings, P. A. (2019). *The trauma sensitive classroom: Building resilience with compassionate teaching.* W.W. Norton and Company.
Johnson, D. W., & Johnson, F. (2009). *Joining together: Group theory and group skills* (10th edition). Allyn and Bacon.
Main, M., & Goldwyn, R. (1984). Predicting rejection of her infant from mother's representation of her own experience: Implications for the abused–abusing intergenerational cycle. *Child Abuse and Neglect, 8,* 203–217.
Main, M., & Solomon, J. (1986). Discovery of an insecure-disorganized/disoriented attachment pattern. In T. B. Brazelton & M. W. Yogman (Eds.), *Affective development in infancy* (pp. 95–124). Ablex Publishing.
Marlowe, M. J., & Hayden, T. (2013). *Teaching children who are hard to reach: relationship driven classroom practice.* Corwin.
O'Connor, E., Collins, B., & Supplee, L. (2012). Behavior problems in late childhood: The roles of early maternal attachment and teacher–child relationship trajectories. *Attachment & Human Development, 14*(3), 265–288.
Ogle, C. M., Rubin, D. C., & Siegler, I. C. (2015). The relation between insecure attachment and posttraumatic stress: Early life versus adulthood traumas. *Psychological Trauma: Theory, Research, Practice, and Policy, 7*(4), 324–332.
Palm, G. (2014). Attachment theory and fathers: Moving from "being there" to "being with." *Journal of Family Theory and Review, 6,* 282–297.
Perry, B., & Szalavitz, M. (2006). *The boy who was raised as a dog: And other stories from a child psychiatrist's notebook: What traumatized children can teach us about loss, love and healing.* Basic Books.
Peterson, K. L. (2014). *Helping them heal: How teachers can support young children who experience stress and trauma.* Gryphon House Inc.
Pianta, R. (2001). *STRS student-teacher relationship scale.* Professional Manual. Odessa: Psychological Assessment Resources, Inc.
Sabol, T., & Pianta, R. C. (2012). Recent trends in research on teacher–child relationships. *Attachment & Human Development, 14*(3), 213–231.
Schunk, D. H. (2001). Social cognitive theory and self-regulated learning. In B. J. Zimmerman & D. H. Schunk (Eds.), *Self-regulated learning and academic achievement: Theoretical perspectives.* Lawrence Erlbaum Associates.
Siegel, D. J., & Bryson, T. P. (2011). *The whole brain child: 12 revolutionary strategies to nurture your child's developing mind.* Bantam Books Trade Paperbacks.
Sorrels, B. (2015). *Reaching and teaching children exposed to trauma.* Gryphon House.

van der Horst, F. C. P., & van der Veer, R. (2010). The ontogeny of an idea: John Bowlby and contemporaries on mother-child separation. *History of Psychology, 13*(1), 25–45.

van der Kolk, B. A. (2014). *The body keeps the score: Brain, mind and body in the healing of trauma.* Penguin Books.

Verschueren, K., Doumen, S., & Buyse, E. (2012). Relationships with mother, teacher, and peers: Unique and joint effects on young children's self-concept. *Attachment & Human Development, 14*(3), 233–248.

Verschueren, K., & Koomen, H. M. Y. (2012). Teacher-child relationships from an attachment perspective. *Attachment and Human Development, 14*(3), 205–211.

Wiebler, L. R. (2013). Developmental differences in response to trauma. In E. Rossen & R. Hull (Eds.), *Supporting and educating traumatized students: A guide for school-based professionals.* Oxford University Press.

Part III

TOOLBOX WITH MORE STRATEGIES TO SUPPORT CHILDREN OF TRAUMA

6

Supporting Reading and Writing Skills for Children of Trauma

This chapter will provide:
- the importance of shared reading experiences and shared storybook readings early in a child's development;
- the significance of strategic reading and comprehension strategies that can be used to support children of trauma in the classroom;
- the effects trauma can have on expressive and receptive language, specifically reading and writing; and
- strategies to implement in the classroom for children of trauma so that they can be successful with their expressive and receptive language skills.

Seminal reading research studies have determined reading is a learned skill that builds on a child's early language and cognitive abilities (Ehri, 1999; Torgesen, 2000; Gaskins et al., 1997; Adams, 1990). Researchers in the reading field have learned the importance of a young child having a strong foundation for several skills before entering a school setting: Emergent literacy skills, shared reading experience, vast vocabulary knowledge, understanding print concepts, the alphabetic principle, and phonetic knowledge are all necessary for literacy in our technological society (Sénéchal et al., 1998; Adams, 1990; Ehri, 1999; Snow et al., 2007; Hill & Diamond, 2012). These skills build a foundation that will lead to stronger achievement in reading, oral language, and written language (Adams, 1990; Chall, 1967; Hill & Diamond, 2012, Ehri, 1999).

Torgesen (2000) notes that a significant group of children who enter school will suffer in regard to weaknesses in preparation for learning to read and they will require instructional interventions. Some children who could be at

> **Sidebar 6.1. Expressive and Receptive Language Development—Revisited**
>
> In chapter 4, we discussed expressive and receptive language development. As a review, expressive language includes speaking and writing, and receptive language includes listening and reading. The focus of chapter 4 was on the struggles children of trauma face in regard to oral language development. In this chapter we will first discuss early reading experiences, including shared storybook reading, the importance of strategic reading strategies, and the ways we can support writing in the classroom. The last two sections will focus specifically on reading and writing struggles for children of trauma and the strategies that can be employed to support their learning in the classroom.

risk may be children who have suffered from some of the following: speech and language disorders, physical or mental disorders, developmental disorders, and/or living in poverty.

One group of children who may also be unprepared may be children of trauma. School-age children suffering from trauma may still struggle with reading and writing skills because of vulnerable executive functioning skills. Furthermore, misidentification of learning disabilities often occurs because of their trauma experiences, and therefore, the proper intervention may not necessarily be provided (Anda et al., 2006; Harris, 2018; Cook et al., 2005).

Previously, expressive and receptive language development was discussed. See sidebar 6.1 for a review of expressive and receptive language development in the classroom.

EARLY READING EXPERIENCES AND SHARED STORYBOOK READING

Language development between birth and kindergarten is a time of immense flourishing as children learn to use communication and expression to provide meaning to their feelings and intentions. Children's vocabulary and language interactions in the home will impact their future language and reading development. Early linguistic interactions and manipulation of language, such as playing with word meanings and jokes, alliterative names, nursery rhymes, word recognition, and so on, can all assist children in their reading comprehension and their writing development (Snow et al., 2007).

Other studies have revealed that toddlers are developing ways of thinking, such as inferring, that could be viewed as a reading comprehension foundational skill (Duke & Carlisle, 2011). Bus (2002) affirms further that book reading may stimulate text understanding because it supports children's knowledge of written language in a contextual framework.

Bus and colleagues (1995) conducted a meta-analysis to test effects of at-home shared book reading on children's language and literacy development in preschool and in school-age children. What they found as a result of reviewing 30 studies was remarkable. First, the home environment directly predicts literacy results in kindergarten and elementary school.

Second, home reading experiences related positively to language growth, emergent literacy skills, phonological awareness, and reading achievement. Results indicate that shared book reading develops concepts about print or print awareness, alphabet knowledge, word reading, and invented spelling (Bus et al., 1995; Phillips et al., 2008; Justice et al., 2005; Duke & Carlisle, 2011).

Concepts about print have been shown to be an earlier predictor for later reading and writing skills (Clay, 2000). Concepts of print are an awareness of "how print works." It encompasses the following understandings: (1) knowledge about print orientation and directionality of print (left to right and top to bottom); (2) distinction between sentences, words, letters, and the spacing in text; (3) understanding that print has meaning and provides a message; and (4) knowledge of the parts of a book, including the author, title, and front and back of the book.

Another benefit is the fact that children who have had the opportunity for shared reading experiences display more interest in reading than do children who lack this early experience (Bus, 2002). Reading books in a shared reading context provides the benefit of exposing children to words they may not be as familiar with or may not use in daily expressive language. Furthermore, it enables children to engage with the complex syntax of written language (Hill & Diamond, 2012).

A study conducted by Bus and van IJzendoorn (1995) explored children's home literacy experiences such as the frequency and quality of book reading and the history of interactive experiences the children shared with their parents. They found that insecurely attached children have negative expectations of parental assistance during reading experiences and thus show less interest in books because enjoyment depends strongly on parental support or help. Insecurely attached children do not explore books as frequently as those children with a better attached relationship with their mother.

Finally, they found the importance for children to have opportunities for active participation during shared reading experiences. Pointing, various vocalizations, changing the tone of voice, and questioning are all valuable to the shared reading experience.

The importance of early storybook reading is evident. Exposure to books provides a rich source of linguistic stimulation for the child that may foster literacy development in a unique way (Bus et al., 1995; Phillips et al., 2008; Justice et al., 2005). Not only should students be exposed at a young age, but also the need for children to read across the developmental lifespan is critical.

For many years, reading researchers Cunningham and Stanovich (1997) and Cunningham and colleagues (2009) have studied how reading can improve fluency, vocabulary, background knowledge, and overall cognitive capabilities. It comes down to this—reading improves reading. The more a person reads, the better they are at it.

Reading is a social-emotional process, and if caregivers are not supportive of this process or are unsure how to interact during storybook readings, training may be warranted to encourage the process of storybook reading engagement. When caregivers have reading difficulties, they themselves may be less likely to expose children to a rich and stimulating linguistic environment. However, many parents aspire for their children from lower socioeconomic status families to "succeed against the odds" (Siraj-Blatchford, 2010).

The research has confirmed that during the early schooling years, reading comprehension development is supported by home and school environments, and thus, schools should support the importance of reading and create a culture of reading that is continued in the home environment (Duke & Carlisle, 2011).

Beyond the early years, picture books should be used in all K–12 classrooms. I, myself, used them many times when I taught high school for 8 years. Why use picture books at a level beyond elementary school? Picture books (fiction and nonfiction), hold attention and engage the reader. Comprehension comes easily because of the support provided by the pictures (Harvey & Goudvis, 2007).

Furthermore, picture books can be used for comprehension strategy instruction and guided discussion of a particular topic. I found that using picture books at the high school level is beneficial for these reasons listed above as well as using them in conjunction with lessons involving the modeling of excellent writing and the teaching of particular writing skills and processes.

RECEPTIVE LANGUAGE: STRATEGIC READING AND COMPREHENSION STRATEGIES

Strategic reading refers to thinking about reading in ways that support learning and understanding of text (Harvey & Goudvis, 2007). Teachers are not just "teaching reading," right? We are truly awakeners. We are teaching readers how to be proficient readers, and this means to be strategic as they read. Strategic readers engage with the text and think critically about what they are reading (Harvey & Goudvis, 2007; McEwan, 2004).

In order for children to develop as strategic readers, educators do need to *explicitly* teach a variety of comprehension strategies which will support students' understanding and subsequent comprehension of text. This is explicit, systematic, and supportive instruction of cognitive strategies taught at all levels and for content and narrative texts and often times call strategic reading instruction (SRI) (McEwan, 2004).

Metacognitive reading strategies like questioning, inferring, summarizing, and predicting have been recognized as effective in teaching reading comprehension (Pressley & Block, 2002; McEwan, 2004). One strategy that has received a lot of attention over the years is the transactional strategy instruction (TSI) approach, which can be used with fictional and/or informational text (Pressley, 2002). The multiple-strategy instruction model has proven effective because of the variety of comprehension strategies that are taught in the TSI approach. Sidebar 6.2 provides the various comprehension strategies that are often taught with this approach.

One additional approach, reciprocal teaching, is an instructional activity in which students become the teacher in a small-group reading session (Oczuks, 2003). Students assume the role of the teacher in leading a discussion regarding the material that was read. Students should be at mastery or near-mastery level for using summarizing, question generating, clarifying, and predicting before using reciprocal teaching. Reciprocal teaching encourages students to think about their own thinking and monitor their comprehension as they read (otherwise known as *metacognition*).

Sidebar 6.2

The following is the repertoire of comprehension strategies that are often taught in the TSI approach (Pressley, 2002):

- questioning;
- summarization;
- prediction;
- visualization;
- activation and use of prior knowledge;
- use of story grammar (fictional texts);
- use of text structures (informational texts);
- thinking aloud;
- understanding when comprehension breaks down;
- personal responses to texts; and
- connections.

"Word attack" or decoding skills are of course another important piece of effective comprehension. Many times, students can be taught to sound out the word, look for context clues, reread, or skip the word. It is hoped that students will learn the "steps" for effective comprehension, including decoding skills, and strategic reading will become common practice when reading a variety of texts. The intent here was to focus on comprehension studies and not phonological processing; therefore, other bodies of research should be explored for a more intimate look at these skills involved in the reading process.

EXPRESSIVE LANGUAGE: COUPLING READING AND WRITING STRATEGIES

Many would argue if you can talk well, writing, as another mode of expressive language, should be a breeze! This could not be further from the truth. Explicit instruction in written expression is needed for many to be successful in the writing process. Written expression can be a struggle for so many because of the fact it is a multifaceted and a multi-step process.

Written expression encompasses lower-level skills like handwriting, spelling, and grammar, and then higher-level skills like idea formulation, topic selection, planning, producing, organizing, revising, and editing text. All of these skills can be found in multiple parts of the brain. The interpretation of words and language can be found in the parietal lobe. If damage or injury occurs to this part of the brain, the person may be unable to write or spell or have impaired reading skills.

The frontal lobe is also associated with speaking and writing. Damage occurring in the frontal lobe can result in fine motor difficulties, speech and language processing difficulties, and thinking difficulties. If written expression is the game, then working memory is the coach of that game. This is the part of the brain that helps us to think and remember at the same time. If you think about all of the processes involved in written expression, working memory is the coach—making sure all the players have equal playing time and play together to win the game.

Because writing is so multifaceted and uses so many systems to work well, many of the struggles we previously discussed in this book can all lead to the struggle of written expression. Written expression is one of the most challenging topics to master or for children to learn—and this is for a child not affected by trauma.

For children to learn the necessary skills for written expression, they will need highly structured, explicit, and systematic instruction. Opportunities for writing practice should be plentiful. Students should be taught to identify various text features and structures when reading and then be taught to transfer their thoughts and comprehension of the text into written work (Culham, 2014; Duke et al., 2012). Lastly, coupling reading with writing helps readers focus their understanding of the text and engage in comprehension processes (Roessing, 2009; Serravallo, 2013).

TRAUMA AND EFFECTS OF EXPRESSIVE AND RECEPTIVE LANGUAGE

As discussed in chapter 4, children affected by trauma will have diminished expressive and receptive language skills (Sylvestre et al., 2015). Research has shown that children of trauma have lower IQs and are underachieving in reading, comprehension, and writing (Stone, 2007). Furthermore, standardized test scores in math and reading can also be significantly lower as well for students living in foster care (Emerson & Lovitt, 2003; Shin, 2003). Studies revealed that children exposed to violence have higher levels of reading problems (as cited in Blackburn, 2008).

As discussed in chapter 1, a high number of ACEs can also place a person at increased risk for later health problems (Harris, 2018). Children who experience ACEs also have an increased possibility of below-average academic skills, including poor literacy and language skills, which as you can imagine, will place them at a substantial risk for overall poor school achievement (Fiscella & Kitzman, 2009; Jimenez et al., 2016).

Reading research has revealed the importance of identifying reading difficulties early in a child's life. Researchers have proven that early delays in reading achievement can lead to long-term reading disabilities (Cunningham & Stanovich, 1997; Shaywitz, 2003; Spira et al., 2005). Quickly identifying and remediating reading difficulties is essential for any student struggling with reading and writing and maybe even more so imperative for children suffering from trauma because, as pointed out previously, trauma can affect cognitive and behavioral development as well as relationship building. Strategic reading is imperative for students to be successful in comprehending and understanding text.

Approximately 4–6% of students have a written expression learning disability (Bernstein, 2013). At times, it is hard to identify a written expression learning disability because so often it is linked with other disabilities, and furthermore written expression difficulties could be a result of trauma. Other difficulties that show comorbidity with written expression could be executive functioning problems like ADHD, depression, and anxiety—which, again, could be a result of significant and/or complex trauma.

Students with written expression difficulties may struggle with organization, sequencing, and coordination. Manifestations of coordination problems that derive from the parts of the brain involving motor skills are also evident in other areas, including drawing, building blocks or puzzles, tying shoes, and dressing. These visual-motor integration skills are tied to executive functioning skills and may require additional assessments and instructions (Fenwick et al., 2015).

STRATEGIES TO SUPPORT READING AND WRITING SKILLS

The following strategies can be used to support a child in the classroom who may be struggling with reading and writing concepts:

- In chapter 4 it was suggested to use graphic organizers to support language development; they can help with written expression as well. Graphic organizers can support children, as they can write about their ideas, and using graphic organizers will support the sequential aspect of the writing task.
- Using the online site PowToon, a video-creation tool, is a wonderful way to use technology to support the reading and writing processes. Using PowToon, students will create a script and then create their PowToon depending on the assignment requirements. Assignments could include: creating an "All about You" video, giving a book talk, providing a literary analysis, or demonstrating parts of a narrative or expository text. There are also a lot of resources online that can support teachers as they decide to use PowToon in the classroom.
- Use picture books! Don't forget, as mentioned earlier, that picture books should be used at all levels to encourage the learning of comprehension strategies and discussion of a particular topic. Not only does it aid in comprehension, but it also could be used as a springboard at the beginning of a lesson and aid in supporting background knowledge. Using picture books during mini-lessons for specific writing skills and processes is beneficial as well. Chapter 7 will further discuss the benefits of using children's literature.
- Harvey and Goudvis (2007) introduce the FQR think sheet to determine importance, ask questions, and respond to text. The FQR sheet has three columns: "Facts," "Questions," and "Response." Students write facts from the texts in the "Facts" column and questions they have in the "Question" column, and lastly in the "Response" column they can write their reactions, feelings, and opinions of the text. This is a powerful tool to have

students engage with the text and use the metacognitive strategies that are so important for strategic reading.
- A multisensory teaching approach is an excellent strategy to use for all children and can also specifically benefit children affected by trauma. A multisensory approach is a technique to help a child learn through more than one sense. Most of the time when teaching, we use a visual and auditory approach. Using two other senses involving touch (tactile) and movement (kinetic) will help the child's brain remember information more easily. Sometimes referred to as VAKT (visual, auditory, kinesthetic, and tactile), these activities are extremely helpful as students hear, see, trace, and write. Here are a few possible activities:
  - Shaving cream can be used! Squirting shaving cream on a cookie sheet and having students practice saying and writing the letters will involve the VAKT strategy.
  - Using fabrics stretched on an embroidery hoop is another way students can practice tracing letters or "writing" their spelling words (and it is not as messy as shaving cream)! Different fabrics can be used like satin, velvet, fleece, or terry cloth.
  - Using a zip-top bag with paint or hair gel mixed with food coloring and/or glitter is another sensory tool that can be used to implement a multisensory approach or the VAKT technique.
- Using content-area journals (subject areas could include science, social studies, or math) can help all students with their writing. Another benefit of using content journals for children of trauma is that when using a personal or a dialogue journal, many times children of trauma are worried they may expose something they are not ready to reveal. A content journal is focusing on the subject content and not the student. Journaling can also be used as a way for students to summarize opinions or reflect on what they know prior to a lesson, or what they learned after the lesson.
- Another way to incorporate writing in the classroom is to write about classroom experiences as they happen and writing about observable behaviors. The Language Experience Approach (LEA) was covered in chapter 4 and provides children with the opportunity to create a story and detail an event that they all experienced. It could be used following a read aloud, after students have conducted research, or following a hands-on activity. Observable behaviors could be which playground equipment is used the most at recess or which school lunches are enjoyed the most. Again, this is a different type of writing and can benefit all students in learning how to collect data and use that data in a writing that will benefit them in the future.
- There are a lot of technology devices that can also support someone who may have difficulties with reading and writing. Recording pens are great to

record thoughts so that you don't forget ideas before you finish writing. A student can then play it back to remind themselves of their thoughts. Audio versions of books are also helpful to listen to stories and aid in comprehension. There is also a reading pen that can scan a line of text and read it to the student.
- As previously discussed, Carol Dweck's work with growth versus fixed mindsets should also continue in the literacy classroom. During literacy instruction, building a growth mindset while increasing students' knowledge of literacy strategies and practices (e.g., learning new vocabulary, decoding skills, writing skills, etc.) should be used as they discuss challenges with reading and how they overcame them (Morrow et al., 2019). The literacy CAFE system developed by Boushey and her team (2020) focuses on *c*omprehension, *a*ccuracy, *f*luency and *e*xpanding vocabulary and is one system that can be used while implementing a growth mindset approach. The CAFE system provides teachers with a way to maximize student understanding of these important components for successful reading and discuss the pitfalls posed by specific literacy tasks. Focusing on the strategies the students can use to support them and then reflecting on their progress can complement teaching literacy strategies and using the growth mindset technique to benefit all learners.
- Teaching students to use symbols to code as they read can aid in comprehension of material. Students will interact with text as they engage in coding and again is a key component of being a strategic reader. Anchor charts can be placed in the classroom as a key for students to refer to while reading. Of course, we want to ensure that using these symbols is supporting their comprehension and not hindering their thought process. Some examples of coding, per Harvey and Goudvis (2007), include:
  - R: reminds me of;
  - !: surprising information;
  - *: key idea;
  - ?: question; and
  - L: new learning.

REFERENCES

Adams, M. J. (1990). *Beginning to read: Thinking and learning about print*. MIT Press.

Anda, R. F., Felitti, V. J., Bremner, J. D., Walker, J. D., Whitfield, C., Perry, B. D., Dube, S. R., & Giles, W. H. (2006). The enduring effects of abuse and related adverse experiences in childhood. A convergence of evidence from neurobiology and epidemiology. *Child: Care, Health and Development, 32*(2), 253–256.

Bernstein, J. H. (2013). Process analysis in the assessment of children. In L. Ashendorf, R. Swenson, & D. Libon (Eds.), *The Boston process approach to neuropsychological assessment: A practitioner's guide* (p. 300). Oxford University Press.

Blackburn, J. F. (2008). Reading and phonological awareness skills in children exposed to domestic violence. *Journal of Aggression, Maltreatment & Trauma, 17*(4), 415–438.

Boushey, G. & Behne, A. (2020). *The CAFE book: Engaging all students in daily literacy assessment and instruction.* 2nd ed. Stenhouse Publishers.

Bus, A. G. (2002). Joint caregiver-child storybook reading: A route to literacy development. In S. B. Neumann & D. K. Dickinson (Eds.), *Handbook of early literacy research.* (pp. 179–189). Guilford Press.

Bus, A. G., & van IJzendoorn, M. H. (1995). Mothers reading to their three-year-olds: The role of mother-child attachment security in becoming literate. *Reading Research Quarterly, 40*, 998–1015.

Bus, A. G., van IJendoorn, M. H., & Pellegrini, A. (1995). Joint book reading makes for succession learning to read: A meta-analysis on intergenerational transmission of literacy. *Review of Educational Research, 65*, 1–21.

Chall, J. (1967). *Learning to read: The great debate.* McGraw-Hill.

Clay, M. (2000). *Concepts about print.* Heinemann.

Cook, A., Spinazzola, J., Ford, J., Lanktree, C., Blaustein, M., Cloitre, M., DeRosa, R., Hubbard, R., Kagan, R., Liautaud, J., Mallah, K., Olafson, E., & van der Kolk, B. (2005). Complex trauma in children and adolescents. *Psychiatric Annals, 35*(5), 390–398.

Culham, R. (2014). *The writing thief: Using mentor texts to teach the craft of writing.* International Reading Association.

Cunningham, A. E., & Stanovich, K. E. (1997). Early reading acquisition and its relation to reading experience and ability 10 years later. *Developmental Psychology, 33*(6), 934–945.

Cunningham, A. E., Zibulsky, J., Stanovich, K. E., & Stanovich, P. J. (2009). How teachers would spend their time teaching language arts: The mismatch between self-reported and best practices. *Journal of Learning Disabilities, 42*, 418–430.

Duke, N. K., Caughlan, S., Juzwik, M. M., & Martin, N. M. (2012). *Reading and writing genre with purpose in K–8 classrooms.* Heinemann.

Duke, N., & Carlisle, J. (2011). The development of comprehension. In M. Kamil, P. D. Pearson, E. B. Moje, & P. P. Afflerbach (Eds.), *Handbook of reading research* (pp. 199–228). Routledge.

Ehri, L. (1999). Phases of development in learning to read words. In J. Oakhill & K. Beard (Eds.), *Reading development and the teaching of reading: A psychological perspective* (pp. 79–108). Blackwell Publishers.

Emerson, J., & Lovitt, T. (2003). The educational plight of foster children in schools and what can be done about it. *Remedial and Special Education, 24*(4), 199–203.

Fenwick, M., Kubas, H. A., Witzke, J. W., Miller, D. C., Maricle, D. E., Harrison, G. L., Macoun, S. J., & Hale, J. B. (2015). Neuropsychological profiles of written expression learning disabilities determined by concordance-discordance model criteria. *Applied Neuropsychology: Child, 5*(2), 83–96.

Fiscella, K., & Kitzman, H. (2009). Disparities in academic achievement and health: The intersection of child education and health policy. *Pediatrics, 123*(3), 1073–1080.

Gaskins, I. W., Ehri, L. C., Cress, C., O'Hara, C., & Donnelly, K. (1997). Procedures for word learning: Making discoveries about words. *The Reading Teacher, 50*, 312–327.

Harris, N. B. (2018). *The deepest well: Healing the long-term effects of childhood adversity.* Houghton Mifflin Harcourt.

Harvey, S., & Goudvis, A. (2007). *Strategies that work: Teaching comprehension for understanding and engagement.* Stenhouse Publishers.

Hill, S., & Diamond, A. (2012). Family literacy in response to local contexts. *Australian Journal of Language and Literacy, 36*(1), 48–55.

Jimenez, M. E., Wade, R., Lin, Y., Morrow, L., & Reichman, N. E. (2016). Adverse experiences in early childhood and kindergarten outcomes. *Pediatrics, 137*(2), 1–9.

Justice, L. M., Skibbe, L., Canning, A., & Lankford, C. (2005). Pre-schoolers, print and storybooks: An observational study using eye movement analysis. *Journal of Research in Reading, 28*(3), 229–243.

McEwan, E. K. (2004). *Seven strategies of highly effective readers: Using cognitive research to book K–8 achievement.* Corwin Press.

Morrow, L. M., Dougherty, S. M. & Tracey, D. H. (2019). Best practices in early literacy. In L. M. Morrow & L. B. Gambrell (Eds.), *Best practices in literacy instruction.* Guilford.

Oczuks, L. (2003). *Reciprocal teaching at work: Strategies for improving reading comprehension.* International Reading Association.

Phillips, L. M., Norris, S. P., & Anderson, J. (2008). Unlocking the door: Is parents' reading to children the key to early literacy development? *Canadian Psychology/ Psychologie Canadienne, 49*(2), 82–88.

Pressley, M. (2002). Comprehension strategies instruction: A turn-of-the-century status report. In C. C. Block & M. Pressley (Eds.), *Comprehension instruction: Research-based best practices* (pp. 11–27). Guilford Press.

Pressley, M., & Block, C. C. (2002). Summing up: What comprehension instruction could be. In C. C. Block & M. Pressley (Eds.), *Comprehension instruction: Research-based best practices* (pp. 383–392). Guilford Press.

Roessing, L. (2009). *The write to read: Response journals that increase comprehension.* Corwin.

Sénéchal, M., LeFevre, J., Thomas, E., & Daley, K. (1998). Differential effects of home literacy experiences on the development of oral and written language. *Reading Research Quarterly, 33*, 96–116.

Serravallo, J. 2013). *Independent reading assessment: Fiction and nonfiction.* Scholastic.

Shaywitz, S. (2003). Overcoming dyslexia: A new and complete science-based program for reading problems at any level. Knopf.

Shin, S. H. (2003). Building evidence to promote educational competence of youth in foster care. *Child Welfare, 82*(5), 615–632.

Siraj-Blatchford, I. (2010). Learning in the home and at school: How working-class children 'succeed against the odds'. *British Educational Research Journal, 36*(3), 463–482.

Snow, C. E., Porche, M. V., Tabors, P.O., & Harris, S. R. (2007). *Is literacy enough? Pathways to academic success for adolescents.* Paul H. Brookes.

Spira, E. G., Bracken, S. S., & Fischel, J. (2005). Predicting improvement after first-grade reading difficulties: The effects of oral language, emergent literacy and behavior skills. *Developmental Psychology, 41*(1), 225–234.

Stone, S. (2007). Child maltreatment, out-of-home placement and academic vulnerability: A fifteen-year review of evidence and future directions. *Children and Youth Services Review, 29*(2), 139–161.

Sylvestre, A., Bussières, È.-L., & Bouchard, C. (2015). Language problems among abused and neglected children: A meta-analytic review. *Child Maltreatment, 21*(1), 47–58. https://doi.org/10.1177/1077559515616703.

Torgesen, J. K. (2000). Individual differences in response to early interventions in reading: The lingering problem of treatment resisters. *Learning Disabilities Research & Practice, 15*, 55–64.

7

The Healing Power of Children's Literature

> This chapter will provide:
> - definitions and a brief history of bibliotherapy;
> - the benefits of bibliotherapy for children but especially those children affected by trauma;
> - ways to implement bibliotherapy in the classroom and in counseling sessions; and
> - book lists to support selection of quality literature to use in whole-group, small-group, and one-on-one settings.

We learned from the previous chapter that reading is an active experience in which students can interpret the story and thus engage with the text. Moreover, children who grow up in unpredictable environments, such as child victims of domestic violence or children experiencing trauma, often need direct instruction in strategic reading to help them approach text in a purposeful manner (Craig, 2008; 2016).

Literature can be used in all classrooms to help teachers connect with their students and open the doors for discussion on tough, realistic topics and should be used at all levels of schooling. "Books specifically focusing on a topic such as divorce, or going to kindergarten, as well as those that concentrate on specific social or emotional skills such as managing anger or handling fear are a significant part of most early childhood book collections and adds significant value to their intellectual and social-emotional development" (Peterson, 2014, p. 139).

In this chapter, we will explore the term *bibliotherapy* as well as the ways this process can be implemented in the classroom. The use of literature circles in this process will also be discussed. Lastly, there will be various book lists provided that will include children's literature for various ages and traumatic events to build resilience.

A BRIEF HISTORY OF BIBLIOTHERAPY

There are many definitions of *bibliotherapy*, and the process used to implement bibliotherapy has progressed over time. At first, reading was used to support people who were in emotional distress. While this is still the case, there are more uses for bibliotherapy than originally thought.

The term *bibliotherapy* is a relatively new term, but the use of reading as a means to change human behavior was recognized and used in Greek and Roman times (Jack & Ronan, 2008; Shechtman, 2009; Hendricks et al., 1999). The term *bibliotherapy* was first used in a 1916 issue of *Atlantic Monthly* in an article by Samuel Crothers. Crothers discussed a technique of prescribing books to patients who needed help understanding their problems, and he labeled the technique *bibliotherapy* (Myracle, 1995). Crothers (1916) states:

> I don't care whether a book is ancient or modern, whether it is English or German, whether it is in prose or verse, whether it is a history or a collection of essays, whether it is romantic or realistic. I only ask, "What is its therapeutic value?" (p. 292)

During World War I, librarians and laypersons involved in organizations such as the Red Cross and Salvation Army established libraries in Army hospitals. The belief at the time was that soldiers and veterans who participated in reading were "diverted or nourished in some mysterious way" (cited in Jack & Ronan, 2008).

Following the first World War, national and local library organizations became more actively involved in the process of bibliotherapy, with hospital library committees established and standards for hospital libraries proposed. In fact, in 1923, a librarian by the name of Sadie P. Delaney instituted a formal bibliotherapy process at a Veterans Affairs (VA) hospital for the first time and later wrote an article about this advancement titled, "The Place of Bibliotherapy in a Hospital" (Jack and Ronan, 2008).

One of her suggestions was that the opportunity to read in a hospital could also be a source of healing. In 1936, the idea of using bibliotherapy with children was introduced by Bradley and Bosquet (1936), who suggested the use of books for children with behavioral and personality disorders.

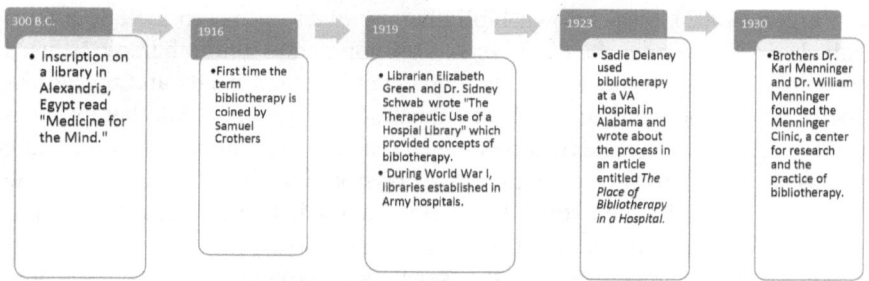

Figure 7.1 Timeline of the evolution of bibliotherapy. *Source:* Colleen Lelli

In 1938, Louise Rosenblatt, a well-known researcher in the field of reading, identified the benefits of bibliotherapy. She noted that as the reader interacts with the characters in a text, they are able to put themselves in another place; evaluate the feelings, needs, and aspirations of others; and extend awareness beyond their family and community. Rosenblatt also recognized that literature is a vehicle for the child to reflect on common experiences shared by others.

In 1945, librarian Clara Kircher prepared and published a book titled *Character Formation Through Books: A Bibliography*. She furthered Rosenblatt's thoughts by stating that it was her belief that the active involvement in reading and solutions contained within the storyline could help children with their own emotional dilemmas. In 1949, Caroline Shrodes's landmark dissertation, titled *Bibliotherapy: A Theoretical and Clinical Experimental Study*, described the human response to literature. She identified phases of bibliotherapy: identification and projection, abreaction and catharsis, and, lastly, insight and integration (Hendricks et al., 1999). These are some of the phases still used today and will be discussed in further detail below.

Figure 7.1 contains the timeline for pertinent information and more of the evolution of bibliotherapy.

Defining *Bibliotherapy* Today

Today, *bibliotherapy* is simply defined as the use of books to help people solve problems (Forgan, 2002); another definition is a technique that uses literary sources to help individuals resolve complex problems (Sullivan & Strange, 2002). By using literature, students can understand themselves, realize that they are not alone, and see hope in their struggles (Leininger et al., 2010). While exploring the literature, students can receive information about solving problems, try possible solutions, and learn strategies to manage their anxiety and stress (Leininger et al., 2010).

Forgan (2002) breaks down bibliotherapy even further to include a term called *developmental bibliotherapy*. Developmental bibliotherapy is used to help students use books for various developmental needs and to address social and emotional issues as they occur. This type of bibliotherapy uses guided reading as an interaction between readers' personalities and literature (Cook et al., 2006). For example, in a classroom setting, teachers will read selected books with their students and build a link between difficult situations and the story they are reading (Leininger et al., 2010).

The goal of bibliotherapy in this sense is to provide guidance for future development by providing expectations of how to deal with similar problems in the future. Another type of bibliotherapy, *clinical bibliotherapy*, was defined by Cook and colleagues (2006): It takes place in a structured setting and is facilitated by a counselor, therapist, or psychologist to treat individuals experiencing serious emotional or behavioral problems.

Bibliotherapy has been used outside of school settings and in a variety of fields, including the health field, library science, psychology, and social work. In fact, in London, England, bibliotherapists offer sessions using a questionnaire and follow-up questions, and then a reading list or "prescription" is provided that meets the needs of the reader. This form of "affective bibliotherapy advocates for the restorative power of reading fiction" (Dovey, 2015).

Children experience a wide range of problems that can hinder their development and can lead to long-term problems (Jackson, 2006). We are aware of the impact ACEs can have on children and the other struggles any child could encounter, such as social belonging issues, self-esteem difficulties, and problem-solving difficulties.

Using bibliotherapy is simply using books to support children with their struggles. Teachers do not need to be counselors or clinical psychologists to implement bibliotherapy. Language arts teachers are usually well-versed in the literature that is available and have an understanding of child development. With that said, the best approach would be to implement a community effort in consultation with the librarian, school counselor or psychologist, and others who may know the reader(s).

Caroline Shrodes (1949) provided a theory that many have followed to understand the way readers pass through specific stages during the bibliotherapy process (Morawski, 1997; Jackson, 2006). The first stage is identification, where the reader makes a connection with a character in the book. The reader is aware of the parallels between their own life and the life of the character presented in the text. "Examining the behaviors and related motives of another individual can act as a transition into the exploration of one's own perceptions and actions" (Morawski, 1997, p. 247).

The second stage identified is catharsis. At this level, under a safe environment, a reader will experience emotions and reveal similarities between characters' lives and their own lives. This allows the reader to gain new perspective on their own problems. The last stage, insight, is a result of catharsis. Here, the reader—after being freed from emotional tension—is willing to discuss possible solutions for a problem. At this point in time, they may be able to understand their own motivations after empathizing with the character and the plot provided in the given text.

Later, two other frameworks will be provided to implement bibliotherapy in the classroom that provide further direction with ties to educational strategies and activities that can be implemented as a result of reading the book(s) chosen.

The Benefits of Bibliotherapy

Using books and implementing bibliotherapy can benefit children in a number of ways. Books that deal with the same issues that children are facing may help students to gain insight into their personal problems and may perhaps guide them to a remedy for their problems (Forgan, 2002). The students can use the characters from the story to discuss topics or issues that may otherwise be difficult for them to talk about openly. Reading teachers and classroom teachers have the ability to break many emotional barriers by reading aloud children's literature related to social problems and allowing children to respond to the text through teacher-guided conversations.

If a teacher knows or suspects that a child is experiencing some type of problem, stress, or crisis, an adjustment in instruction can be made by using literature. Today, more than ever, with the rise of mental health, violent shootings, and other significant traumas in our world, using books to help children heal is imperative. See table 7.1 for examples of children's socioemotional issues or traumas that could be helped by bibliotherapy.

Using literature in this matter allows children to develop perspective taking. Perspective taking is the ability to understand what other people think,

Table 7.1. Examples of Traumas or Emotional Issues Children May Experience

Domestic violence	Physical abuse	Sexual abuse	Bullying
Substance abuse	Mental illness	Anxiety	Body image
Failure	Homelessness	Sexual orientation	Problem solving
Divorce or family discord	Friendship issues	Depression	Self-esteem
Grief	Chronic illness	Economic hardship or poverty	Anger

feel, and know (Peterson, 2014). As a developmental process, perspective taking allows children to better understand their own difficult experiences but also the experiences of others (Peterson, 2014). Stories that provide developmentally appropriate information when devastating events occur—like domestic violence, damaging storms, violence in the community—will give children the opportunity to understand the events and also will provide them with information about how others respond and cope with these events (Peterson, 2014).

This is supported even further as a result of recent research using fMRI brain scans (Mar, 2011). We now understand the ways the brain is stimulated

Story:
- Does the story convey a story that is realistic, empathetic, and sensitive to the child with the disability or life difficulty and thereby encourages a positive attitude?
- Does the story enable the child to resolve the conflict or problem?
- Are there various conflicts for children to explore?
- Is the story simple yet believable?

Characters:
- Do the characters represent people from a variety of cultural groups?
- Do "good" characters reflect a variety of backgrounds?
- Are there female and male characters? Are females as well as males depicted in leadership roles?
- Does the story discuss characters feelings, needs or goals?
- Do characters show coping skills?

Themes:
- Does the story offer a difficult topic to think about, to question and to consider?
- Are values being explored?
- Are there lessons to be learned?
- Does the story emphasize success rather than failure?

Settings:
- Are cultural settings represented realistically?

Illustrations:
- Are diverse populations represented?
- Are characters realistically and genuinely represented?
- Do the illustrations avoid reinforcing societal stereotypes?

Other considerations:
- Will the story encourage discussions?
- Are children exposed to multiple perspectives and values?
- Is the story age appropriate to ensure children can understand what is presented?
- Are certain terms used negatively?
- Does the book promote empathy and not pity?

Figure 7.2 Checklist for evaluating children's literature. *Source:* **Colleen Lelli**

as a result of self-medicating with great books (Dovey, 2015; Mar, 2011). Mar's (2011) study demonstrates that when people read about a character and their involvement in an experience, neurological regions of the brain are activated as if the readers were experiencing the event themselves. He concludes that we draw on the same neural networks when we are reading narratives and when we are guessing others' feelings, known as Theory of Mind (Baron-Cohen et al., 1985), and similarly what Peterson (2014) describes as perspective taking.

Another benefit of bibliotherapy is exposing students to various books and to introduce a love for reading. Many at-risk students may not engage regularly in recreational reading, and this will provide students with quality literature while helping them cope with their struggles and their real-life situations. Chances of success, academically and socially, increase while using good literature because the students are able to meaningfully connect to their own lives (Prater et al., 2006; Peterson, 2014).

In addition to classroom teachers, reading teachers should be aware of quality children's literature that can be used in the classroom to help children with any emotional issues. See figure 7.2 for a checklist that can be used when evaluating children's literature. When a book draws attention to social issues that are relevant to the experiences of young children, it offers a means of understanding in a way that is less intimidating than having a classroom discussion or lesson on a topic (Peterson, 2014). In collaboration with a guidance counselor, a teacher can help implement bibliotherapy or use books to create conversations in the classroom about sensitive issues in either full-group or small-group instruction.

IMPLEMENTING BIBLIOTHERAPY

Bibliotherapy is most effective when conducted as an interactive process in which guided discussions are used to achieve therapeutic goals (Cook et al., 2006), and it is a process that has a plan, an opening, a discussion, and a closing. To implement bibliotherapy, Cook and colleagues (2006) identify four steps: (1) identify the problem, situation, behavior, or skill to be acquired; (2) select an appropriate work of literature; (3) present the literature; and (4) follow up the reading with a discussion.

The literature that is presented should provide accurate information and should not provide a student with unrealistic expectations or a false sense of hope. The developmental level and reading level of the child must be considered when choosing appropriate literature and presentation of the literature. Prater et al. (2006) identify a 10-step process that expands on the four-step process identified by Cook and colleague (2006). See sidebar 7.1 for the steps in this process.

Sidebar 7.1. Steps in the Bibliotherapy Process

Prater et al (2006) designed a 10-step process to implement bibliotherapy:

1. Develop rapport, trust, and confidence with the student: *Teachers should develop rapport, trust, and confidence by getting to know their students throughout the school year.*
2. Identify other school personnel who may assist: *A collaborative approach is also paramount when working with students and especially students of trauma. Other personnel could include a social worker, counselor, school psychologist, or nurse.*
3. Solicit support from the student's parents or guardians: *Parents or guardians can provide important information and should be considered collaborative partners.*
4. Define a specific problem the student is experiencing: *Teachers are not counselors, nor should they take on that role, but again collaborating with professionals who can counsel and design a protocol to support the child in the classroom with the specific problems they are encountering is important.*
5. Create goals and activities to address the problem: *A plan of action with specific goals and activities is prudent. The creation of the goal will guide the instruction.*
6. Research and select books appropriate for the situation: *Prater and colleagues (2006) suggest that the books selected should be based on (1) appropriateness for developmental age and reading ability of the child, (2) the portrayal of the topic of interest or difficulty (e.g., mental illness), (3) character portrayal realism, and (4) literary quality.*
7. Introduce the book to the student: *Consideration for confidentiality and sensitivity for the student should be made when introducing the book.*
8. Incorporate reading activities: *Various reading strategies can be implemented during this step for students to comprehend and make connections with the texts. A few strategies that could be implemented include: Directed Reading and Thinking Activity (DRTA), concept maps, double-entry journals, Question Answer Relationship (QAR), and jigsaw strategy.*
9. Implement post-reading activities: *Art and writing projects can be effective post reading activities. Technology can be used as a way for students to express their feelings while making a connection to the text. For example, Pixton is a web-based program that allows students to create their own comic strip.*
10. Evaluate the effects of bibliotherapy on the student: *Once the bibliotherapy process is complete, teachers need to evaluate the steps and the process to gauge the effectiveness of the process.*

Forgan (2002) suggests using the following four elements for the framework of bibliotherapy: (1) prereading, (2) guided reading, (3) post-reading discussion, and (4) a problem-solving/reinforcement activity. These elements are not new for educators familiar with best practices in reading-based instruction. Social workers or counselors may not be as familiar with the use of these steps.

During prereading, selection of materials is made, and students' background knowledge is activated to help them link their past experiences to the present book content. Many sound reading strategies can be used at this point, such as KWL charts, Venn Diagrams, and prediction questions.

Books are read aloud during the guided-reading phase. At this point, the entire story should be read without asking too many questions. Discussions of students' own experiences should be left up to the counselor/teacher's discretion. After the reading of the story, students could write their reactions in a journal.

During post-reading discussion, some researchers have suggested first having students retell the plot and evaluate character feelings and any situations that occurred (Forgan, 2002; Cook et al., 2006). Students will discuss the story and possibly will be able to relate it to their situation during this phase. The facilitator must plan for a follow-up discussion beginning with simple questions and leading to more critical ones. The facilitator must allow for interpretation, analysis, synthesis, and evaluation of the characters, problems, and solutions or coping strategies from the story line (Cook et al., 2006).

Rosenblatt (1982; 1991; 2005) suggests using open-ended questions and remarks in discussions that help guide students' attention back toward the reading event and keep the experiential elements in mind. Reading logs and double-entry notebooks with journal starters can help to connect the text with the reader's prior knowledge (Galda & Aimonette-Liang, 2003). Other activities that can encourage an aesthetic stance include reenacting the story or dramatizing, illustrating, writing in dialogue journals, webbing, and imaging, having children design their own book with their own storyline and characters (Galda & Aimonette-Liang, 2003).

During the problem-solving stage, Forgan (2002) suggests implementing a strategy called I SOLVE. I SOLVE stands for: *I*dentify the problem; *S*olutions to the problem; *O*bstacles to the solutions; *L*ook at the solutions again (choose one); *V*ery good—try it!; and *E*valuate the Outcome. Using this strategy is good teaching practice. Having teachers collaborate with other staff members to present effective strategies—such as I SOLVE—is beneficial to staff and students.

BOOK LISTS TO SUPPORT SELECTION OF QUALITY LITERATURE

The following books lists are provided to support educators, counselors, and administrators to use quality literature when providing bibliotherapy in the classroom or in counseling sessions. Some of the literature can be used in a full-class setting or a small-group setting, while others should be reserved during times of one-on-one counseling sessions. It's imperative as educators that we recognize we are not counselors, and so if students need counseling, a collaborative approach needs to be employed within the school system.

Addressing sensitive topics like homelessness, divorce, death, or any other delicate topics should be handled with care. If you are discussing a sensitive topic in a large group and you are aware a student has faced or is facing that situation, you might want to converse with the student prior to the reading of the story in the full group. Confidentiality is key, and discussing these issues with guidance counselors or social workers as part of a collaborative approach is paramount.

Table 7.2 provides a list of books for preschool, elementary, and young adult students who have been affected by trauma. The books in table 7.3 are recommended for adolescents who have experienced difficult times like a trauma, but they also can be used to provide support and build resilience and determination as a result of a challenging situation.

Table 7.2. Books to Support Children of Trauma

Child Witness of Violence or Trauma		
Coman, C. (1997)	What Jamie Saw	(Elementary–Middle)
Holmes, M. (2000)	A Terrible Thing Happened: A Story for Children Who Have Witnessed Violence or Trauma	(Preschool–Elementary)
Moses, M. (2015)	Alex and the Scary Things: A Story to Help Children Who Have Experienced Something Scary	(Preschool–Elementary)
Shuman, C. (2003)	Jenny Is Scared: When Sad Things Happen in the World	(Preschool–Elementary)
Watts, G. (2009)	Hear My Roar: A Story of Family Violence	(Elementary)

Child Abuse

Roberts, W. (1988)	*Don't Hurt Laurie*	(Upper Elementary–Middle)
King, K. (2008)	*I Said No! A Kid-to-kid Guide to Keeping Private Parts Private*	(Elementary)

Foster Care

DeGarmo, K. (2014)	*A Different Home: A New Foster Child's Story*	(Preschool–Elementary)
Gilman, J. (2008)	*Murphy's Three Homes: A Story for Children in Foster Care*	(Preschool–Early Elementary)
Kasza, K. (1996)	*A Mother for Choco*	(Preschool–Early Elementary)
Wilgocki, J. (2002)	*Maybe Days: A Book for Children in Foster Care*	(Preschool–Early Elementary)

Death

Benjamin, A. (2015)	*The Thing About Jellyfish*	(Upper Elementary–Middle)
Cochran, B. (2007)	*The Forever Dog*	(Preschool–Early Elementary)

Divorce

Blume, J. (2014-Republished)	*It's Not the End of the World*	(Upper Elementary–Middle)
Masurel, C. (2003)	*Two Homes*	(Preschool–Early Elementary)

Special Needs

Doering-Tourville, A. (2010)	*My Friend Has Autism*	(Elementary)
Edwards, K. (2006)	*The Memory Keeper's Daughter*	(Young Adult/Adult)
Moore-Mallinos, J. (2008)	*My Friend Has Down Syndrome*	(Elementary)
Piccoult, J. (2010)	*House Rules*	(Young Adult/Adult)

Feelings

Annunziata, J. (2009)	*Sometimes I'm Scared*	(Elementary School)
Bang, M. (1999)	*When Sophie Gets Angry—Really, Really Angry*	(Preschool–Elementary)
Cain, B. (2001)	*Double Dip Feelings: Stories to Help Children Understand Emotions*	(Preschool–Elementary)
Curtis, J. (2007)	*Today I Feel Silly: And Other Moods That Make My Day*	(Preschool–Elementary)
Dismondy, M. (2008)	*Spaghetti in A Hot Dog Bun: Having the Courage to Be Who You Are*	(Preschool–Elementary)
Karst, P. (2000)	*The Invisible String*	(Preschool–Early Elementary)
McCloud, C. (2006)	*Have You Filled a Bucket Today? A Guide to Daily Happiness for Kids*	(Elementary)

Table 7.3. Adolescent Literature for Children of Trauma Building Resilience and Determination

Anderson, L. H. (2011). *Speak*.	*Speak* is the story of Melinda, who was raped at a party and needs to find her own voice to speak up for herself.
Bell, C., & Lasky, D. (illustrator). (2014). *El Deafo*.	In this graphic novel memoir, Cece Bell narrates her life with hearing loss and wearing a hearing aid and the difficulty she had making friends. After some difficulties, she is able to embrace her hearing loss and the power of the Phonic Ear.
Bradley, K. (2016). *The War That Saved My Life*.	10-year-old Ada is never allowed out of her apartment because her mother is embarrassed by Ada's twisted foot. Ada sneaks out to join her brother, Jamie, who was sent to London to escape the war. They stay with a woman named Susan who takes care of them lovingly, but will they have to go back to their mother and their home after the war?
Erskine, K. (2011). *Mockingbird*.	Caitlin is a young girl with Asperger's Syndrome. Her brother was recently killed in a school shooting, and Caitlin is trying to learn to live without him.
Forman, G. (2010). *If I Stay*.	Mia is in a coma after a family car crash. As the only survivor, Mia needs to consider if she will fight or live without her parents and brother. Mia's life struggles and the relationships she has with friends and families are shared.
Lai, T. (2013). *Inside Out and Back Again*.	Hà immigrates from Saigon to America. This story chronicles her first year in America and the changes, dreams, and healing that must occur as a result of being in her new home and new culture.
Lost, L. (2016). *The Fireproof Girl*.	Sophie was abandoned, abused, and neglected. When her only friend, Cole Hunter, is murdered, Sophie goes on the search to find his killer.
Murphy, J. (2017). *Dumplin'*.	Willowdean Dickson (nicknamed "Dumplin'" by her mother) has always been comfortable with her body. As she begins dating and suffering from comments made from kids at school, she starts to doubt her self-image. To regain her confidence, she enters the Miss Teen Blue Bonnet Pageant.
Palacio, R. J. (2012). *Wonder*.	August Pullman was born with a facial difference, and for the first time he is attending school. The story is told from multiple perspectives: August, his classmates, and others. An uplifting story about the power of acceptance and compassion.
Park, L. (2011). *A Long Walk to Water: Based on a True Story*	Told from alternating points of view of two 11-year old children in Sudan, one from 2008 and the other from 1985. The girl (Nya) and the boy (Salva) share their stories of resilience and survival as they try to find their families and find a safe place to live.

Paulsen, G. (2006). *Hatchet*	Brian Robeson is traveling to visit his newly divorced father and still reeling from the fact that he holds a secret about his mother's infidelity. When the plane crashes and Brian is the only survivor, he must learn to survive in the wilderness.
Rawls, W. (1996). *Where the Red Fern Grows*	Billy has longed to own two dogs, and he was able to purchase two dogs after he saved his own money. Word travels that this trio are the finest hunting team. Suddenly, tragedy strikes, and Billy learns how resilience can build after unbearable despair.

REFERENCES

Baron-Cohen, S., Leslie, A. M., & Frith, U. (1985). Does the autistic child have a "theory of mind?" *Cognition, 1*, 37–46.

Bradley, C., & Bosquet, E. S. (1936). Uses of books for psychotherapy with children. *American Journal of Orthopsychiatry, 6*, 23–31.

Cook, K., Earles-Vollrath, T., & Ganz, J. (2006). Bibliotherapy. *Intervention in School and Clinic, 42*, 91–100.

Craig, S. (2008). *Reaching and teaching children who hurt: Strategies for your classroom*. Paul H. Brookes Publishing Company.

Craig, S. (2016). *Trauma-sensitive schools: Learning communities transforming children's lives, K–5*. Teachers College Press.

Crothers, S. (September 1916). A Literary Clinic. *The Atlantic Monthly, 118*(3), 291–301.

Dovey, C. (2015, June 9). Can reading make you happier? *New Yorker*. https://www.newyorker.com/culture/cultural-comment/can-reading-make-you-happier

Forgan, J. (2002). Using bibliotherapy to teach problem solving. *Intervention in School and Clinic, 38*, 75–82.

Galda, L. & Aimonette-Liang, L. (2003). Literature as experience of looking for facts: Stance in the classroom. *Reading Research Quarterly, 38*, 268–275.

Hendricks, C. G., Hendricks, J. E., & Cochran, L. L. (1999). Literacy conversations: Family, school, community. In R. J. Telfer (Ed.), *Using literacy conversations for healing: The significant conversationalists*. American Reading Forum Online Yearbook.

Jack, S. J., & Ronan, K. R. (2008). Bibliotherapy: Practice and research. *School Psychology International, 29*, 161–182. DOI: 10.1177/0143034308090058

Jackson, M. N. M. (2006). *Bibliotherapy revisited: Issues in classroom management. Developing teachers' awareness and techniques to help children cope effectively with stressful situations*. Mangilao, Guam: M-m-mauleg Publishing. (ERIC Document Accession No. ED501535)

Kircher, C. J. (1945). *Character formation through books: A Bibliography*. The Catholic University of America Press.

Leininger, M., Dyches, T. T., Prater, M. A., Heath, M. A., & Bascom, S. (2010). Books portraying characters with obsessive compulsive disorder: Top 10 list for children and young adults. *Teaching Exceptional Children, 42*, 22–28.

Mar, R. A. (2011). The neural bases of social cognition and story comprehension. *Annual Review of Psychology, 62*, 103–134. https://doi.org/10.1146/annurev-psych-120709-145406

Morawski, C. M. (1997). A role for bibliotherapy in teacher education. *Reading Horizons, 37*, 243–259.

Myracle, L. (1995). Molding the minds of the young: The history of bibliotherapy as applied to children and adolescents. *The Alan Review, 22*.

Peterson, K. L. (2014). *Helping them heal: How teachers can support young children who experience stress and trauma* (1st edition). Gryphon House.

Prater, M. A., Johnstun, M. L., Dyches, T. T., & Johnstun, M. R. (2006). Using children's books as bibliotherapy for at-risk students: A guide for teachers. *Preventing School Failure, 50*, 5–13.

Rosenblatt, L. M. (1938). *Literature as exploration*. D. Appleton-Century.

Rosenblatt, L. M. (1982). The literary transaction: Evocation and response. *Theory Into Practice, 21*, 268–277.

Rosenblatt, L. M. (1991). Literature S.O.S.! *Language Arts, 68*, 444–448.

Rosenblatt, L. M. (2005). *Making meaning with texts: Selected essays*. Heinemann.

Shechtman Z. (2009) Using bibliotherapy as a preventive intervention in the classroom. In Treating child and adolescent aggression through bibliotherapy. The Springer Series on Human Exceptionality. Springer, New York, NY. https://doi.org/10.1007/978-0-387-09745-9_9

Shrodes, C. (1949). Implications for psychotherapy. In R. J. Rubin (Ed.), *Bibliotherapy sourcebook* (pp. 96–122). The Oryx Press.

Sullivan, A. K., & Strange, H. R. (2002). Bibliotherapy in the classroom using literature to promote the development of emotional intelligence. *Childhood Education, 79*(2), 74–80, DOI:10.1080/00094056.2003.10522773

8

Creating Trauma-Sensitive Schools

The Importance of Mental Health Awareness and Positive School Climate

> This chapter will provide:
> - the importance of mental health awareness and a comprehensive approach for supporting all students in schools;
> - suggestions for implementation of best practices to build positive school climate;
> - social-emotional learning practices and curriculum that can be incorporated as a schoolwide approach and within classrooms;
> - ways to use the Universal Design for Learning (UDL) framework to implement positive school climate and trauma informed practices; and
> - specific definitions of a mandated reporter and resources to understand mandated-reporting roles in each state.

Students are in our classroom every day, and those who do not feel safe will find it extremely difficult to learn. There are other students who have struggles like not eating enough or not having a permanent home or living with a parent with mental health illnesses. According to Becker and Luthar's (2002) seminal research, stress in the classroom can be reduced, and promotion of social-emotional growth can exist by the creation of a nurturing environment. Recent research supports this finding.

Basch (2011) concludes that healthier students are better learners, and Kenyatta (2012) states that teachers' perceptions of their students can positively or negatively influence how students view themselves. Furthermore, not only do students need ongoing support from their classroom teachers, but also barriers to learning must be addressed in schoolwide and districtwide initiatives. A whole-school approach is necessary to ensure students feel supported and connected socially, emotionally, and physically by all school staff.

Despite all of the adverse, stressful experiences students face today, as of 2020, only 11 states encourage or mandate staff training on the effects of trauma. Most states have failed to implement a comprehensive plan to address student well-being (Keierleber, 2019). Because of these studies, it is imperative that we create a culture of a positive school climate and recognize the importance of mental health awareness.

In this chapter, we explore ways to create trauma-sensitive schools, including the importance of mental health awareness, a positive school climate, using a social emotional learning approach and a Universal Design for Learning framework (Meyer et al., 2014), and knowledge regarding mandated-reporting guidelines.

THE IMPORTANCE OF MENTAL HEALTH AWARENESS TO CREATE TRAUMA-SENSITIVE EDUCATION ENVIRONMENTS

Positive mental health is critical to learning in addition to social and emotional development and a trauma-sensitive approach. Up to 20% of kids living in the United States show signs or symptoms of a mental health disorder in a given year, and the numbers seem to be increasing from previous documented studies (Ghandour et al., 2019). In addition, mental health concerns increase for students who live in adverse environments (World Health Organization, 2004).

Many of these students who need mental health services will not be identified, and furthermore, many will not receive the necessary services. Regardless of whether students are receiving treatments, these children are still in the school system. They will face many problems related to succeeding in school the environment, such as behavior problems, low achievement, absenteeism, substance abuse, and quitting school.

Mental health includes psychological, emotional, and social well-being. This also includes how we handle stress, our mindset, relationships with others, and the choices we make. It is for this reason one could argue that schools and teachers could play a definitive role in identifying children with mental health needs and helping those children succeed in school. Unfortunately, teachers are overtaxed with the responsibilities of running a classroom, including assessing, educating students, and using the given curriculum. This is only the short list of the responsibilities educators face every day. Some feel that "schools are not in the mental health business as it is their mission to educate" (Adelman & Taylor, 2013).

While this may be true, many state officials and advocates are recognizing the importance for pre-service and in-service teachers to be trained on how to identify and respond to mental health problems they are encountering and noticing with their students. In a study conducted by Reinke and colleagues (2011), only 34% of teachers surveyed felt they had the skills they needed to identify and support students with mental health needs.

A comprehensive approach to mental health is needed to support children, and educators who can support these vast needs are essential. The family, teacher, social worker, counselor, principal, special education teacher, school psychologist, school nurse, and community agencies all play a role in supporting a child who is struggling with mental health needs. It is imperative that school systems evaluate and find the best approach for their setting.

What are some ways schools can try to help children with mental health challenges? First, we can start talking about the importance of recognizing mental health difficulties in our school curriculums. This will help reduce the stigma that mental health seems to carry. The more open we are as educators, the easier it will be to identify any difficulties when the symptoms arise. A comprehensive approach regarding mental health needs to be adopted, much like we implemented discussions of physical health or healthy eating in school curricula.

Second, creating a cool-down room, a calm area, or a peace corner for students will provide them the opportunity to regain or regulate their emotions. Many schools allow this for students who have this addressed in an Individualized Education Program (IEP) or a 504 plan, but this can work for all students. Students who use this benefit are learning how to regulate their emotions appropriately, and staff can note how often a student may be using the calm room. This can help educators identify the students who may need mental health support.

Some teachers have a cool-down station in their class. It could have a comfortable chair or desk that is away from the group. A cool-down box with things like puzzles, Silly Putty, stress balls, coloring books, and crayons can all be used by a child who needs a few moments to themselves.

Next, mental health training should be a full school effort. All educators, bus drivers, cafeteria, playground, before- and after-care personnel, and office support staff should undergo mandatory training in regard to mental health. Training should include an understanding of risk factors for their students, trauma-informed care, signs of mental health issues, along with the proper support for educators and staff to support students at risk in getting the help they need. Many state governments are now mandating that teachers and anyone working closely with children should be trained in mental health first aid. This is imperative and a step in the right direction to lessen the stigma surrounding mental health and ensure students receive the help they need.

Lastly, like trauma-informed care, mental health support does take the support of the community. Engaging with outside agencies to gain their expertise for training and programming is key. Connecting with parents can also benefit students who may be faced with mental health challenges.

In the following section, positive school climate will be explored to better understand how an organizational structure and positive mindset can change the culture of a school to benefit all students and their learning styles and needs.

POSITIVE SCHOOL CLIMATE: A TRAUMA-SENSITIVE APPROACH

According to the National School Climate Council (NSCC), "School climate reflects the norms, goals, values, interpersonal, relationships, teaching, learning and leadership practices and organizational structure that comprise school life" (National School Climate Standards, 2009, p. 2). Recent research has proven that learners want and need to be safe and happy, and it also shows that when school members feel safe, valued, and cared for, engaged learning increases and staff retention improves (Cohen, 2006; Cohen et al., 2009; Fredricks et al., 2004; Reinke et al., 2011).

In other words, all school community members are respected, and students, families, and school staff work together to promote a positive school climate. There is a set of norms and values that guides everyone in a pursuit of a common purpose.

Sidebar 8.1. Positive School Climate Impact

A positive school climate can:

- influence positive learning and enhance academic achievement while closing the achievement gap;
- decrease teacher and staff turnover and therefore lead to commitment from staff to the organization and/or school;
- escalate teacher and staff satisfaction;
- increase academic achievement in low-performing schools, including increasing graduation rates;
- foster effort and productivity;
- improve collegial and collaborative activities that lead to better communication; and
- increase the motivation and energy of staff and students.

Source: National School Climate Standards (2009).

A huge gain that can result because of positive school climate is higher academic achievement (National School Climate Standards, 2009; Shindler et al., 2016). For this reason alone, many educators can appreciate the encouraging results of positive school climate. A positive school climate supports all learners, and the students we see struggling the most, those with high ACE scores, will benefit the most from a positive school climate. See sidebar 8.1 for a list of encouraging outcomes that can result from a positive school climate.

As schools implement positive school climate, guidance needs to be used to ensure best practices and that these practices are implemented with care. The NSCC developed the National School Climate Standards (2009) and provided a framework of five standards to support effective school climate improvement. Sidebar 8.2 outlines these standards.

Many schools are finding the Multi-Tiered Systems of Support (MTSS) framework successful for implementing a trauma-sensitive approach. MTSS

Sidebar 8.2. Framework for a Positive School Climate

The following National School Climate Standards were created by the NSSC in 2009 to better inform administrators and educators and provide a research-based framework as they implement a positive school climate culture.

1. The school community has a shared vision and plan for promoting, enhancing, and sustaining a positive school climate.
2. The school community sets policies specifically promoting (a) the development and sustainability of social, emotional, ethical, civic, and intellectual skills, knowledge, dispositions, and engagement; and (b) a comprehensive system to address barriers to learning and teaching and reengage students who have become disengaged.
3. The school community's practices are identified, prioritized, and supported to (a) promote the learning and positive social, emotional, ethical, and civic development of students; (b) enhance engagement in teaching, learning, and school-wide activities; (c) address barriers to learning and teaching and reengage those who have become disengaged; and (d) develop and sustain an appropriate operational infrastructure and capacity-building mechanisms for meeting this standard.
4. The school community creates an environment where all members are welcomed, are supported, and feel safe in school: socially, emotionally, intellectually, and physically.
5. The school community develops meaningful and engaging practices, activities, and norms that promote social and civic responsibilities and a commitment to social justice.

Source: National School Climate Standards (2009).

can be used to serve all students while proactively identifying students who are at risk through universal screening and then implementing evidence-based interventions for students in need both academically and behaviorally. Jennings (2019) states, "Folding trauma sensitive strategies into an existing system of supports across the school or district can facilitate system-wide implementation for a more comprehensive approach" (p. 66). The three levels of intervention for academic or behavior challenges include:

- Tier I is primary prevention or universal for all students. This includes core instruction for a full class using social-emotional learning (SEL) curriculum, reading curriculum, or a schoolwide Positive Behavioral Intervention and Support (PBIS) framework. PBIS is an approach to promote positive behavior, improve school safety, and promote a positive school climate. The core belief of PBIS is that schools teach kids about behavior just as they would teach any subject. It is believed that children need to know what the behavioral expectations are in the classroom and within the school setting.
- Tier II is secondary prevention and is for selected at-risk students. Some supports in place at this level could be small-group SEL training, self-monitoring, or small-group reading instruction.
- Tier III is tertiary prevention for students with significant challenges who have not responded to tier I or tier II interventions and supports. Students with emotional or trauma difficulties may need cognitive behavioral counseling, a functional based assessment and intervention, or family therapy.

Improving school climate effectively for longevity takes care in planning and implementing. Administration, staff, and the community need to work together. Therefore, a list of other resources (table 8.1) is provided to support administration, educators, and the greater community in creating effective positive school climate change. These resources and frameworks can be used by school systems who want to assess and/or change their school climate to ensure a positive school climate for all stakeholders.

Table 8.1. Positive School Climate Frameworks

Framework	Authors	Summary
Conditions for Learning	American Institutes for Research (2014). *ESSIN Task 31, Subtask 2: Position paper on School Climate Survey (SCLS) content*. Author.	American Institute for Research provids an assessment to measure school climate.

Framework	Authors	Summary
Maryland Safe and Support Schools (MDS³)	Bradshaw, C. P., Waasdorp, T. E., Debnam, K. J., & Johnson, S. L. (2014). Measuring school climate in high schools: A focus on safety, engagement, and the environment. *Journal of School Health, 84*(9), 593–604.	This assessment examines the effectiveness of PBIS.
National School Climate Council (NSCC) framework	National School Climate Center. (2016). *School climate.* http://www.schoolclimate.or g/climate	The NSCC reviewed more than 200 school climate studies and considered relationships, safety, teaching and learning, and environmental structure as part of a positive school climate.
Safe and Supportive Schools Model	National Center on Safe and Supportive Learning Environments (NCSSLE). (2016). *School climate.* https://safesupportivelearning.ed.gov/safe-and-healthy-students/school-climate	This model uses the NSCC framework to design a broader model.
Whole Child Initiative	ASCD. (2016). *ASCD's whole child approach.* http://www.ascd.org/whole-child.aspx	Although the Whole Child Approach is not a positive school climate framework, it is a model that instead places the child at the center and addresses school climate from the perspective of the healthy, holistic development of children.

The Intersection of School Climate and Social-Emotional Learning

Using comprehensive approaches like the MTSS framework to support children of trauma within a school and classroom is ideal. Chafouleas and colleagues (2016) note that using a trauma-sensitive approach should accomplish the following: prevent further adverse events; help individuals who are displaying adverse effects of trauma to recover; and lastly, avoid retraumatizing students who have encountered adverse events.

Throughout this chapter, it's been stated that strong leadership in the administration and teacher-leaders is imperative to develop and implement school policies. Meaningful professional developments for staff and strong relationships among and between educators and mental health professionals will also provide a strong, safe, and trauma-sensitive school approach.

There is a body of research that suggests the importance of the intersection between school climate and social-emotional learning (SEL) to ensure a positive trauma-sensitive school and classroom approach. *SEL* has been defined as the process through which children and adults understand and manage emotions, set and achieve positive goals, feel and show empathy for others, establish and maintain positive relationships, and make responsible decisions (Collaborative for Academic, Social, and Emotional Learning [CASEL], 2019). SEL is integrated within classrooms and throughout the school community through partnerships with families and community members and aligned with targeted services for students who need them, as discussed using the MTSS framework.

CASEL (2019) suggests that systemic SEL is promoted across multiple contexts every day and incorporates five core competencies to support students in a welcoming learning environment:

1. Self-awareness: Learners understand their strengths (emotions, goals, values) and approach learning with a "growth mindset" and optimism.
2. Self-management: Learners are able to manage stress, control impulses, persevere through challenges, and achieve goals.
3. Social awareness: Learners are able to understand the perspective of others and empathize and feel compassion for others, including persons with diverse backgrounds and culture.
4. Relationship skills: Learners are able to use tools to form relationships with others, such as being able to positively communicate, listen well, cooperate with others, and negotiate conflict and social pressure when necessary.
5. Responsible decision-making: Learners are able to make positive choices regarding personal behavior, attitudes, and social interactions based on social norms and safety.

Figure 8.1 depicts the competency wheel that integrates these five competencies within the classroom, school, community, and home. *Learning* was intentionally placed in the term *social and emotional learning* by CASEL to show that the acquisition of skills is a learning process and the school environment can be effective in this process.

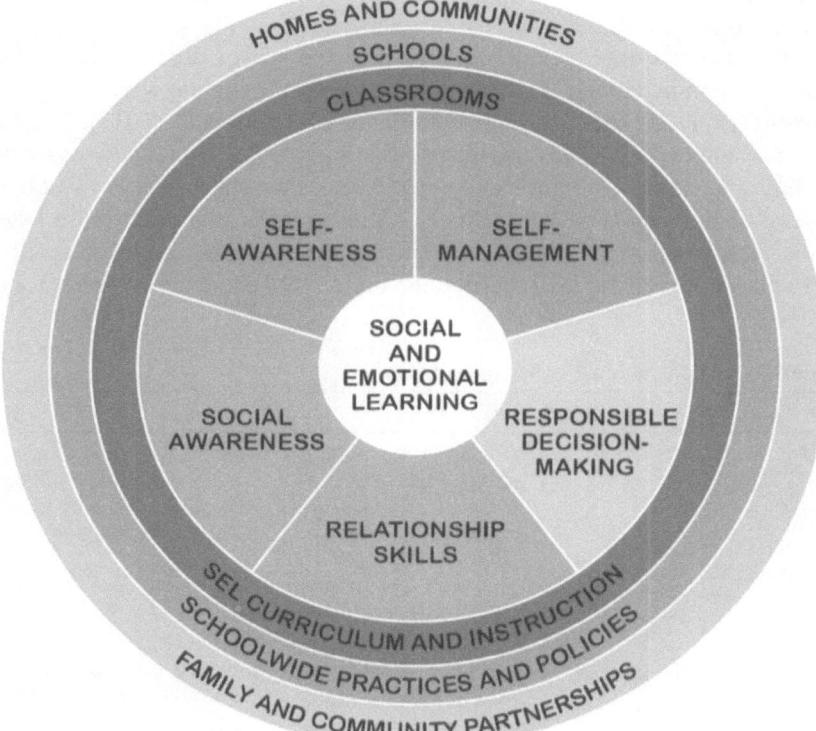

Figure 8.1 CASEL competency wheel. *Source:* CASEL

Some argue that a misinterpretation of SEL is the belief that social-emotional competencies can be taught like other academic subjects. Some researchers believe that a better approach would be to consider using a developmental perspective instead and be more strategic about the competencies to prioritize and approach at each stage. This thinking has led to some using the term *social-emotional development* (SED) (Noam & Triggs, n.d.; Jones et al, 2017). Consider this thinking as you learn more about SEL and SED and compare various frameworks and approaches.

SEL practices should be implemented as a schoolwide approach, within classrooms, and as a framework among educators, families, and communities. Schools that are characterized by safe, supportive, and inclusive interactions can then in turn better implement strategies to combat bullying, harassment, and violence, which would further help build social-emotional learning competencies in individuals and create optimal conditions for learning (Berg et al., 2017). To create a positive social environment, students and staff need to have social and emotional competencies, and a positive school climate generates the conditions to build these competencies.

Because of the interactions between positive school climate and social-emotional competencies, SEL programs and school climate approaches can borrow from each other and share common goals (Berg et al., 2017). CASEL is one example of an SEL framework that can be used in school systems. Table 8.2 includes resources and frameworks that can be used by school systems to implement SEL in schools. (Other frameworks exist; those listed in the table are just a few that have been widely adopted in designing SEL curricula.) Furthermore, SEL curriculum options are presented in textbox 8.1.

Table 8.2. Social-Emotional Learning Frameworks

Framework	Authors	Summary
Employability Skills Model	Association for Career and Technical Education. (2016). *What is "career ready"?* https://www.acteonline.org/wp-content/uploads/2018/03/Career_Readiness_Paper_COLOR.pdf	Skills necessary to be successful in the workforce are taught in the education or workplace setting.
Partnership for 21st Century Model	Partnership for 21st-Century Learning. (2007). *Framework for 21st-century learning.* http://www.p21.org/about-us/p21-framework	Provides a list of skills and knowledge students need to be successful in the workforce and life in general. Also included are curricula, assessments, professional development, and learning environment resources.
Building Blocks Model	Stafford-Brizard, K. (2015). *Building blocks for learning: A framework for comprehensive student development.* Turnaround for Children. https://www.turnaroundusa.org/what-we-do/tools/building-blocks/	A framework that provides the skills necessary to develop the whole child, including the social, emotional, motivational, and cognitive skills for every learner. The overarching skills include: healthy development, perseverance, mindsets for self and school, school readiness, and independence and sustainability.

Framework	Authors	Summary
Clover Model	Program in Education, Afterschool & Resiliency. (2015). *The Clover Model.* http://www.pearweb.org/about/Clover.html	The Clover Model highlights four essential elements for people of all ages to learn and develop, including active engagement, assertiveness, belonging, and reflection.
Strive Framework	Measuring Social and Emotional Learning. (2013). *Beyond content: Incorporating social and emotional learning into the Strive Framework.* Strive Network. http://www.strivetogether.org/sites/default/files/images/Strive%20Together%20Volume %20I.pdf	The Strive Framework focuses on five social and emotional learning competencies: academic self-efficacy, growth mindset, grit and perseverance, emotional competences, and self-regulated learning and study skills.
Collaborative for Academic, Social, and Emotional Learning (CASEL) Program Guides	CASEL. (n.d.). *CASEL program guides.* https://casel.org/guide	The Collaborative for Academic, Social, and Emotional Learning (CASEL) offers two systematic framework guides (preschool and elementary edition, and middle and high school edition) for evaluating the quality of social and emotional programs.

Textbox 8.1. Social Emotional Learning (SEL) Curriculum

The following list includes several effective, research-proven, evidence-based social emotional learning programs.

1. Empowering Education: Provides a K–8 curriculum that covers the five core competencies from the Collaborative for Academic, Social, and Emotional Learning (CASEL). A sample of the curriculum is provided on their website: https://empoweringeducation.org.
2. Second Step: A PK–8 curriculum that includes skills in impulse control, showing empathy, anger and emotional management, problem solving, and developing self-regulation skills. Scope and sequence charts for grade spans are provided on their website: https://www.secondstep.org/second-step-social-emotional-learning.

(continued)

Textbox 8.1. continued

3. Roots of Empathy: This curriculum is for grades K–8 and has shown effectiveness in reducing levels of aggression, raising social/emotional competence, and increasing empathy: https://rootsofempathy.org.
4. Responsive Classroom Approach: A K–5 curriculum that includes morning meetings, three to five positively stated school rules, problem-solving strategies in class or small groups, and using positive redirecting language and logical consequences for misbehavior: https://www.responsiveclassroom.org.
5. Positive Action: This curriculum can be used in middle and high school as it is a K–12 curriculum. Positive Action promotes intrinsic interest in learning and encourages cooperation among students: https://www.positiveaction.net.
6. Toolbox by Dovetail Learning: Toolbox is a K–6 curriculum that encourages social justice through empathy, resilience, self-mastery, empathy for self and others, and understanding: https://www.dovetaillearning.org.

STRATEGIES TO SUPPORT SOCIAL-EMOTIONAL LEARNING

Beyond incorporating an SEL curriculum, there are a few ways an educator could build practices within their classroom throughout the day to support SEL. Concepts that are reinforced using these strategies include accountability, self-awareness, social awareness, and relationship building.

- A check-in period at the start of each day will make personal connections with each student. A high five or special handshake as each student walks into the classroom is one way to accomplish this.
- During morning meeting, each student can say how they feel or use a chart with various facial expressions to circle or point to how they are feeling that day. Also, classroom jobs can also be given during this time, and this will teach responsibility and ownership of tasks.
- Nurturing a culture of kindness is an excellent way to develop and understand each other's feelings. *Have You Filled a Bucket Today?* by Carol McCloud is an excellent book to explain how using words of kindness can have an effect on those around us.
- Using anchor charts can help to teach social-emotional skills. Different topics could include problem solving, being a good friend, or being a good listener.
- Cooperative learning games can be used to promote building positive relationship skills in the classroom. They will build social-emotional skills and also build community in the classroom.

UNIVERSAL DESIGN FOR LEARNING: A TRAUMA-SENSITIVE APPROACH

Another framework to consider when building a trauma-sensitive environment is Universal Design for Learning (UDL). Traditionally UDL is a framework to improve and optimize teaching and learning for all people (CAST, n.d.). UDL is beneficial because it minimizes barriers and maximizes learning for all students.

UDL is based on insights from the science of *how* people learn. The framework is flexible in how students access and engage with material and curricula, and it provides a plethora of ways for students to show what they know. The framework and premise have basically remained the same since the 1990s when Meyer and colleagues (2014) first introduced the UDL framework, but now we can see how useful it can also be for students of trauma.

Now that we have the definition of *UDL*, let's break it down to truly understand UDL as a framework and subsequently how it can support children affected by trauma. When we look at the word *universal* in this sense, it means that the curriculum is used and understood by everyone—this includes children affected by trauma. This means training everyone in the school community on trauma-informed practices and using the same universal vocabulary. Bus drivers, cafeteria workers, secretaries, janitors, and even parents should be included in the training in addition to teachers and administrators. As educators, we can attest to the fact that student populations are diverse, and students come to school with their own unique backgrounds, needs, and ways of learning.

The next word is *design*. Initially, universal design was an architectural concept. In the field of architecture, it is a design approach that increases the potential for developing a better quality of life for a wide range of individuals. It is a design process that enables and empowers a diverse population by improving human performance, health and wellness, and social participation (Steinfeld & Maisel, 2012).

Curb cuts are a perfect example of a design that is helpful for a person in a wheelchair, but it also is beneficial for someone pushing a baby in a stroller. In education and in the classroom, designing curriculum and classroom activities that meet the needs of all students, improves their learning and social participation, and considers their health and wellness is vital in the UDL framework.

Lastly, the word *learning* in the UDL framework applies to the three brain networks:

Table 8.3. Universal Design for Learning (UDL) Framework and Children of Trauma

UDL for Learning Guidelines	Key Questions	Implementation in the Classroom for Children of Trauma
Provide Multiple Means of Engagement (Provide options for recruiting interest, sustaining effort, and persistence and self-regulation)	How can I engage all students in my class?	Create an accepting and supportive climate.
	How can I support students as they develop the ability to self-regulate?	Create class routines.
		Implement alerts and previews that can help learners anticipate and prepare for changes in activities, schedules, and novel events.
		Vary the pace of work and availability of time-outs or timing or sequence of activities.
		Provide models, scaffolds, and feedback to assist learners in developing internal controls and coping skills by using real-life situations or simulations.
		Identify checkpoints for long-term projects to evaluate effort and persistence as students work toward their long-term goal.
Provide Multiple Means of Representation (Provide options for perception, language, and symbols and comprehension)	How can I present information in ways that reach all learners?	Display information in varied formats such as graphs, tables, video, other visuals, and so on.
	How do I support students in understanding new information?	Consider learners that learn better via auditory or visual means. Provide transcripts for videos or auditory clips, and provide auditory cues for concepts.
		To support comprehension, provide support for unfamiliar syntax by highlighting transition works; use concept maps to bridges ideas between new concepts and previously learned concepts.
		Transferring and generalization are necessary when learning new concepts; using checklists, organizers, sticky notes, and graphic organizers can provide scaffolds to connect new information with prior knowledge.

UDL for Learning Guidelines	Key Questions	Implementation in the Classroom for Children of Trauma
Provide Multiple Means of Action and Expression (Provide options for physical action, expression and communication, and executive functions)	How can I offer purposeful options for students to show what they know?	Use other tasks besides paper-and-pencil tasks. Some examples are using social media and interactive web tools, using physical manipulatives, using dance/movement, film, music, drawing, illustrations, and so on.
	Am I providing students access to assistive technology, and have I considered other methods besides paper-and-pencil tasks for students to show their knowledge?	To support planning and strategy development, provide checklists, planning templates for understanding, and a schedule of steps. Embed various prompts like "show and explain your work" and "stop and think before acting."
		Use multiple tools for construction and composition such as spellcheckers, grammar checkers, text-to-speech software, calculators, preformatted graph paper, providing sentence starters, story webs, concept-mapping tools, and various virtual and concrete mathematics manipulatives.

Source: Adapted from http://udlguidelines.cast.org.

1. the recognition network (the *what* of learning), which is supported by Multiple Means of Representation;
2. the affective network (the *why* of learning), which is supported by the Multiple Means of Engagement; and
3. the strategic network (the *how* of learning), which is supported by the Multiple Means of Action and Expression.

These core principles of UDL—Multiple Means of Engagement, Multiple Means of Representation, and Multiple Means of Action and Expression—have expanded into a series of checkpoints that can be applied to curriculum design, assessment, and teaching. This also provides an opportunity for educators to look at curricula from a trauma-informed lens to ensure that children are not being retraumatized.

For instance, if a video will be viewed in class with content involving war and the resulting fleeing or immigration of residents, the teacher should prepare the class ahead of time about the movie. This could be upsetting for some students if they immigrated to the United States because of a war in their own country or perhaps for a child who may have lost a loved one because of a military action.

Table 8.3 provides further information about each of these principles with a few implementation guidelines or accommodations that can be used for each of the three core principles in the UDL framework: Engagement, Representation, and Perception. (Further options can be found at http://udlguidelines.cast.org.)

THE RESPONSIBILITY OF A MANDATED REPORTER

Sadly, as educators, we know that children are not always safe and at times are abused and/or neglected. Because children could be considered a vulnerable population, it is important as educators for us to recognize our duty to keep them safe and healthy.

Mandated reporting means that teachers, social workers, principals, other school personnel, physicians, nurses, childcare providers, counselors, therapists, law enforcement officers, or people working with children are legally obligated to report any signs of abuse or neglect. Abuse could be physical or sexual. A mandated reporter is protected from civil or criminal liability. Non-mandated reporters are also protected as long as the report was made in good faith. Each state has a list of professionals who are required to report and the standards for making such reports. The Child Welfare Information Gateway provides a list for each state, who is required to report, and the standards for making that report: https://www.childwelfare.gov/pubPDFs/manda.pdf#page=1&view=Introduction.

Another term used is *institutional reporting*, which refers to a mandated reporter who is working or volunteering in a hospital, school, or childcare center and has knowledge that leads them to suspect that abuse and/or neglect has occurred. Within institutions, internal policies and procedures mandate that the person report the abuse to the head of the institution, which then leads to the reporting to Child Protective Services or other authorities. It is imperative that educators are aware of the proper reporting procedures in their state and at their place of employment.

If suspected abuse is not reported by a mandated reporter, states do have a range of penalties or criminal charges, such as misdemeanors and monetary fines as well as imprisonment. The Child Welfare Information Gateway provides a database of search topics related to child abuse and neglect, child welfare, and the statutes for each state: https://www.childwelfare.gov/topics/systemwide/laws-policies/state.

REFERENCES

Adelman, H. S., & Taylor, L. (2013). Mental health in schools and public health. *Public Health Rep., 121*(3), 294–298.

Basch, C. E. (2011). Healthier student are better learners: High-quality, strategically planned, and effectively coordinated school health programs must be a fundamental mission of schools to help close the achievement gap. *Journal of School Health, 81*(10), 650–662.

Becker, B., & Luthar, S. (2002). Social-emotional factors affecting achievement outcomes among disadvantaged students: Closing the achievement gap. *Educational Psychologist, 37,* 197–214.

Berg, J., Osher, D., Moroney, D., & Yoder, N. (2017). *The intersection of school climate and social and emotional development.* American Institutes for Research.

CAST. (n.d.). *About Universal Design for Learning.* http://www.cast.org/our-work/about-udl.html#.XT3ULy3MzUo

Chafouleas, S. M., Johnson, A. H., Overstreet, S., & Santos, N. M. (2016). Toward a blueprint for trauma-informed service delivery in schools. *School Mental Health, 8,* 144–162. doi:10.1007/s12310-015-9166-8

Child Welfare Information Gateway. (2019). *Mandatory reporters of child abuse and neglect.* U.S. Department of Health and Human Services, Children's Bureau.

Cohen, J. (2006). Social, emotional, ethical and academic education: Creating a climate for learning, participation in democracy and well-being. *Harvard Educational Review, 76*(2), 201–237.

Cohen, J., Mccabe, L., Michelli, N. M., & Pickeral, T. (2009). School climate: Research, policy, teacher education and practice. *Teachers College Record, 111*(1), 180–213.

Collaborative for Academic, Social, and Emotional Learning (CASEL). (2019). *What is SEL?* https://casel.org/what-is-sel/.

Fredricks, P., Blumenfeld, P., & Paris, A. (2004). School engagement: Potential of the concept, state of the evidence. *Review of Educational Research, 74*, 59–109.

Ghandour, R. M., Sherman, L. J., Vladutiu, C. J., Ali, M. M., Lynch, S. E., Bitsko, R. H., & Blumberg, S. J. (2019). Prevalence and treatment of depression, anxiety, and conduct problems in U.S. children. *The Journal of Pediatrics, 206*, 256–267.

Jennings, P. A. (2019). *The trauma sensitive classroom: Building resilience with compassionate teaching.* W.W. Norton and Company.

Jones, S. M., Brush, K., Bailey, R., Brion-Meisels, G., McIntyre, J., Kahn, J., Nelson, B., & Stickle, L. (2017). *Navigating SEL from the inside out.* Harvard Graduate School of Education. https://www.wallacefoundation.org/knowledge-center/Documents/Navigating-Social-and-Emotional-Learning-from-the-Inside-Out.pdf

Keierleber, M. (2019, January 31). *Despite prevalent trauma, from school shootings to the opioid epidemic, few states have policies to fully address student needs, study finds.* https://www.the74million.org/despite-prevalent-trauma-from-school-shootings-to-the-opioid-epidemic-few-states-have-policies-to-fully-address-student-needs-study-finds/?fbclid=IwAR3XteJOrTSvDTvzTDa3HbvEV9ybAd3lb7YTcBK0BsMn8yZNdn2AHOZQhcU

Kenyatta, C. P. (2012). From perception to practice: How teacher-student interactions affect African American male achievement. *Journal of Urban Learning, Teaching, and Research, 8*, 36–44.

Meyer, A., Rose, D. H., & Gordon, D. (2014). *Universal design for learning: Theory and practice.* CAST Professional Publishing.

National School Climate Standards. (2009). *National School Climate Standards: Benchmarks to promote effective teaching, learning and comprehensive school improvement.* https://ocde.us/EducationalServices/LearningSupports/HealthyMinds/Documents/School%20Climate%20Matters/school-climate-standards-nscc.pdf

Noam, G. G., & Triggs, H. B. (n.d.). *The Clover Model: A developmental process theory of social-emotional development.* https://www.thepearinstitute.org/clover-model-overview

Reinke, W. M., Stormont, M., Herman, K. C., Puri, R., & Goel, N. (2011). Supporting children's mental health in schools: Teacher perceptions of needs, roles, and barriers. *School Psychology Quarterly, 26*(1), 1–13.

Shindler, J., Jones, A. Williams, A. D., Taylor, C., & Cardenas, H. (2016). The school climate-student connection: If we want achievement gains, we need to begin by improving the climate. *Journal of School Administration Research and Development, 1*(1), 9–16.

Steinfeld, E., & Maisel, J. (2012). *Universal design: Creating inclusive environments.* John Wiley & Sons.

World Health Organization. (2004). *Prevention of mental disorders: Effective interventions and policy options: Summary report.* Author. https://apps.who.int/iris/handle/10665/43027

9

Teaching Resilience, Grit, and Determination

This chapter will provide:

- definitions of *resilience, grit,* and *growth mindset* and the ways they are connected to trauma and education.
- exploration of various models and frameworks that can be used in school systems when designing curriculum and lesson plans to teach resiliency, grit, and a growth mindset.
- strategies that can be implemented in the classroom to support students as they develop resiliency, grit, and a growth mindset.

In chapter 8, we explored how to build positive school climates through a trauma-sensitive lens using a UDL approach. Various SEL programs and curriculum were provided to implement in schools and classrooms while maintaining the need for mental health awareness.

Chapter 9 will build on the previous chapter's content by recognizing the importance of building resilience, grit, and a growth mindset for all children but especially those children affected by trauma. The exploration of the use of various strategies that can be employed to further build resilience, grit, and a growth mindset will also be provided.

WHAT IS RESILIENCE?

Resilience, from an experimental perspective, is a perplexing topic to study. Why is it that some who have unsurmountable obstacles, stress, and other threats can "bounce back" but others have difficulty showing resilience

> **Sidebar 9.1. Professor Norman Garmezy**
>
> Dr. Norman Garmezy, a developmental psychology professor from the University of Minnesota, was the first researcher to study resilience in an experimental setting. He traveled the country and focused on schools in economically deprived areas, interviewing principals, nurses, and counselors. Unlike previous studies, his inquiry asked, "Can you identify stressed children who are making it here in your school?" instead of "Can you identify children who are troubled?" (Konnikova, 2016).
>
> Jennings (2019) notes that Garmezy and his colleagues "looked for strength, rather than weakness and found that certain factors appeared to buffer the impacts of adversity. These factors included a personal feeling of autonomy; a sense of control over the environment; and the quality of reactions to the environment, such as the ability to reappraise and self-regulate" (p. 113).
>
> Sadly, Garmezy's work was cut short because of early onset Alzheimer's (Konnikova, 2016), but it paved the way to study resilience and protective factors or "elements of an individual's background or personality that could enable success despite the challenges they faced" (Konnikova, 2016). It's because of his pioneer work and then those who followed that we now know that resilience can be a set of skills that can be taught.

during stressful times? Before we can answer this question, let's take a look at how *resilience* is defined.

Resilience is an important term when we are building a trauma-sensitive school environment because educators can support children as they rebuild or nurture what is called a growth mindset (more on this term later). Resilience has been researched for some time, and one of the first researchers was developmental psychologist Dr. Norman Garmezy. Sidebar 9.1 provides more information about Dr. Garmezy.

The American Psychological Association (APA) (2014) defines *resilience* as the process of adapting well in the face of adversity, trauma, tragedy, threats, or even significant sources of stress. Condly (2006) defines *resilience* as a strong, stress-resistant attitude. Dr. Kenneth Ginsburg (2015) provides yet another definition: "Resilience is about being able to recover from adversity, bouncing back even when life brings you down" (p. 89).

Stress and resilience are intertwined. It's important to note that stress in this sense could refer to family and relationship problems, serious health problems, or workplace and financial stressors. In chapter 1, we discussed positive stress, tolerable or moderate stress, and toxic or chronic stress. As we previously discovered, stress becomes a destructive force that harms our bodies and our minds if it becomes chronic or it is not manageable (Ginsburg & Jablow, 2015).

Both Ginsburg and Jablow (2015) and Southwick and colleagues (2014) recognize the complex construct of resilience and the ways it may be defined differently in the context of individuals, families, organizations, societies, and cultures and across disciplines. Southwick and colleagues (2014) further clarify that resilience could be viewed as a trait, a process, or an outcome.

Another very important point to consider when defining *resilience* is that, as Pietrzak and Southwick (2011) stress, resilience more likely exists on a continuum and may differ across domains of life. This means that one individual may adapt well to stress in the workplace or in school but may have difficulty adapting in personal relationships. Ginsburg and Jablow (2015) provide an excellent metaphor to support the understanding of resilience: "Resilience is similar to buoyancy. When pushed under water, our bodies instinctively rise back up to the surface" (p. 4).

MODELS AND FRAMEWORKS FOR RESILIENCY

John Hopkins University devised a model called the John Hopkins University Model of Human Resistance, Resiliency and Recovery (Kaminsky et al., 2007). In this model *resilience* is defined by using a three-point continuum, as outlined below:

1. Resistance: In this case, *resistance* means to build up immunity in our minds against traumatic experiences that occur in our lives.
2. Resiliency: Resiliency, or the ability to rebound from adverse situations, is the second point on the continuum.
3. Recovery: Lastly, recovery is the ability to return to previous levels of functioning both psychologically and behaviorally after these critical incidents. Family members, educators, or anyone else with whom a child may have a close bond may collaborate in supporting the recovery for the child. (Everly & Firestone, 2013)

The strategic foundation on which this model is built has four distinct areas, which can be found in table 9.1. The strategies provided will align closely with the components of resiliency as noted in The Model of Human Resistance, Resiliency and Recovery. Using the John Hopkins University Model of Human Resistance, Resiliency and Recovery can help educators better understand the elements of resiliency and how these components can be used to build resiliency when children are faced with trauma and adverse experiences in their lives. At the end of this chapter, strategies will be provided to support the teaching of resiliency.

Table 9.1

Foundational Elements	Description
Providing realistic expectations	Prior to a traumatic experience, discuss expectations and coping skills so that a child is better able to predict how they may respond when the event occurs. For example, discussing with a child who may be seeking cancer treatment the way a particular test will be run can help them to alleviate some of the stress. The more that a child is able to imagine how an event or experience may look, sound, feel, and so on, the more likely they will be able to recover.
Fostering group cohesion and social support	Significant individuals in a child's life can provide support and motivation. These individuals could include family, friends, teachers, mentors, and/or coaches. During the school day, educators could have lunch with students to build these relationships; after-school activities are another time that provides opportunities for growing these important connections.
Fostering positive cognitions	Positive cognition is thinking positively. Positive cognition or optimistic thinking can prevent toxic stress and build resilience. Another term that we will discuss later in the chapter, coined by Carol Dweck, is called *growth mindset*.
Self-efficacy and hardiness	Self-efficacy and hardiness are two distinct terms but could also be connected to a positive growth mindset. Self-efficacy is the belief in one's own self that they can achieve the goals they have set for themselves. Hardiness is the ability to view stressful events as challenges and use the opportunity to grow. A child who is able to learn and grow from experiences will find greater successes and manage stressful and traumatic situations.

Adapted from: Everly and Firestone (2013).

Ginsburg and Jablow (2015) use the 7 Crucial C's as a common language about resilience for collaboration among colleagues, community partners, spouses, and so on. Although they do not necessarily note that this is a framework, I believe it could be used as schools and educators think about ways to define and implement resiliency practices. Below are the 7 C's and a brief explanation of each component.

- Competence: Competence involves managing situations and problems effectively. Making responsible choices, trusting one's own judgment, and confronting challenging situations are all skills necessary to develop competence.
- Confidence: As Ginsburg and Jablow (2015) note, "Children who experience their own competence and know they are safe and protected develop a deep-seated security that promotes the confidence to cope with challenges" (p. 25).
- Connection: When children have strong connections with family, friends, mentors, and teachers, they will be less likely to harm themselves and seek other destructive tendencies.
- Character: Children with positive self-worth and confidence have a strong value system and will develop a resilient mindset.
- Contribution: "Children who understand the importance of personal contribution gain a sense of purpose that can motivate them" (Ginsburg & Jablow, 2015, p. 27). A child's competence, character, and connection will be boosted when they contribute to the greater world and their own community.
- Coping: Learning effective coping skills and stress-reduction strategies can help everyone become more resilient but can be extremely helpful to teach young children when resilience is taught.
- Control: Understanding that a person can control their own decisions and actions is a positive mindset perspective. Children who are optimistic about their choices and actions will be resilient and promote growth in their competence and confidence.

These are two frameworks that can be used in school systems as they develop their SEL curriculum and want to include a resiliency-based piece.

ATTACHMENT THEORY AND RESILIENCE

In chapter 5, we reviewed analysis of attachment theory and attachment styles and the ways trauma can interfere with a secure attachment relationship. Interactions between a child and caregiver can influence future relationships throughout a child's lifespan. A positive attachment will help a child develop self-regulation with their emotions and help them accept social support when coping with stress (Jenkins, 2016).

Jennings (2019) further asserts that the development of empathy and compassion can be cultivated and reinforced with a healthy attachment bond. These are emotions and positive attributes that can be further developed in the first attachment relationship, a relationship that is critical for a child to develop resilience. "The quality of care provided during this critical period lays down the neural pathways for the adaptive systems children need to manage stress" (Craig, 2016, p. 81). Trauma or attachment failures can impede resiliency development.

Previously, we also discussed the ways the brain can be affected by adverse experiences. Brain scans of children who were faced with adverse experiences showed a lack of connectivity in areas necessary to create loving relationships (Nakazawa, 2015). This lack of connectivity can lead to a child having little awareness of their own feelings and an absence of understanding of how their own behavior can affect others.

Fortunately, schools have the potential to build and develop resiliency and a growth mindset. "Working with the brain's neuroplasticity, teachers are able to cultivate children's inner strengths, increase their sense of connection with others and improve their ability to self-monitor their behavior" (Craig, 2016). Furthermore, as we also previously learned from Brofenbrenner's theory, schools are social systems that have the potential to support student learning and behavior.

Cefai (2008) notes that resilience is developed in classrooms when caring relationships exist between the teacher and the student, a strong positive community is built in the school and the classroom, students are engaged in meaningful activities, and high expectations are set. All of the literature and the research we have discussed up to this point culminates to the whole idea of building, cultivating, and teaching resiliency. Before we begin to provide some strategies for resiliency, what about the terms *growth mindset* and *grit*? What is a growth mindset? What is grit? How are these terms linked to resiliency?

GROWTH MINDSET AND GRIT: THE TWO GS

What Is Growth Mindset?

Growth mindset is a term that was coined by Carol Dweck (2006) and has received a lot of attention recently in the education field. In her groundbreaking research, Dweck and her colleagues noticed that some students were able to rebound, or show resiliency, while others could not. They noticed some students had a growth mindset while others had a fixed mindset.

Growth mindset, or the understanding that abilities and intelligence can be developed, is a very important concept that can be applied to life in general. "The hand you're dealt is just the starting point for development" (Dweck,

2006, p. 7). People with a growth mindset will thrive on challenges and view failure as a springboard for growth.

Growth mindset can drive motivation and achievement. Providing students with a variety of strategies and then using those strategies would be a growth mindset approach. On the other hand, fixed mindset is the idea that qualities such as creative ability and intelligence are static or cannot be changed. It is also the belief that success is related to intelligence, and instead of striving for success in order to avoid failure, people will give up without trying.

Through research, Dweck was able to prove that providing compliments for abilities, such as "you're so smart" or "you can hit that ball," develop a dependency on external validation. This also led children to believe that either they had the innate ability, or they did not. However, they found that providing accolades for hard work, effort, and perseverance helped to grow resiliency and determination within the children. Furthermore, Dweck was able to prove through scientific evidence, that because the brain is flexible and has plasticity, people's brains change with experience. The brain is able to change, and so can our mindset.

Two other terms that coincide with a growth mindset are the terms *self-efficacy* and *hardiness*. Building off of the research by Albert Bandura (1997), *self-efficacy* is defined as the belief in one's ability to organize and implement a plan required to achieve desired goals. Hardiness is a belief in one's self-efficacy or the opportunity to see challenges as an area of growth (again, growth mindset!) that one tackles with commitment and a sense of purpose.

Bandura (1997) further believes that to build self-efficacy, one must continually perform and surround themselves with others who achieve and work hard. It is also believed that motivational speeches and self-talk can build self-efficacy and optimism.

Growth and fixed mindsets need to be considered as leaders in education and schools. Most recently, Dweck (2015) has reexamined the idea of a growth mindset and felt compelled for educators to recognize that we're all a mixture of fixed and growth mindset, and we will probably always be. After coming to terms with that thought, she then states that if we want to move closer to a growth mindset in our own thoughts and practices, we need to acknowledge and keep in check our fixed mindset thoughts.

Watching for our fixed mindset "triggers" will support us as educators as we encourage our students. Table 9.2 provides positive growth mindset comments you can use with your students.

Table 9.2. Growth vs. Fixed Mindset Statements to Inspire Students

Growth Mindset (do say)	Fixed Mindset (don't say)
"You worked so hard on this project!" (Children will understand the value of their effort.)	"You are so smart." (Don't say this because then children will think intelligence is a fixed quality.)
"Great job trying a new kind of math problem." (Children will understand the value of their effort.)	"Just do your best—not everyone is good at math." (Don't say this because then children will think intelligence is a fixed quality.)
"This answer is not correct. We are going to find some strategies that will support your understanding as you learn this concept." (Being honest with students and showing them that there is always room to grow and learn is a growth mindset. This also teaches them the importance of using strategies to support learning, emphasizing that learning is an intentional process.)	"That's not correct. You need to pay attention more in class. It doesn't seem like you are trying and working hard enough." (A child of trauma may have biological systems [fight, flight or freeze, as one example] interfering from using strategies that would help them learn. They also learn that making mistakes is bad instead of learning and being challenged.)
"You've worked really hard at learning more challenging pieces of music. We should consider an advanced music class for you." (This is teaching students that being challenged is something we value for lifelong learning.)	"You are musically talented. Because you are so good at it, you should take more advanced classes." (Encouraging students to only continue doing what they are good at will lead to students being afraid to take challenges with new activities.)

What Is Grit?

A growth mindset does not just lead to resiliency, but it also leads to possessing what we call *grit*. Angela Duckworth, the University of Pennsylvania professor who coined the term *grit*, like Carol Dweck, was able to prove that intelligence is not necessarily the most important predictor of success. Duckworth studied people in different challenging circumstances, like new teachers in difficult neighborhoods, National Spelling Bee participants, and West Point cadets.

As a result of this research, Duckworth (2016) concludes that grit consists of two components: passion and perseverance. The research on grit proposes that a child's capability to work hard, persevere through struggles, fail, and try again may be the key to long-term success and happiness. "Grit then is a combination of passion, resilience, determination, and focus that allows a person to maintain the discipline and optimism to persevere in their goals even in the face of discomfort, rejection, and a lack of visible progress for years, or even decades" (Williams, n.d.).

One caution we need to consider is that many children of trauma are facing daily adversities. In the classroom, some educators may view these children

> **Sidebar 9.2**
>
> How "gritty" are you? Take the "Grit Scale" test to determine how much passion and perseverance you perceive yourself to have: https://angeladuckworth.com/grit-scale.

as not having grit because they may appear as if they are not trying or not on task. We need to remember, as educators, that these particular students have much more grit than we realize.

In fact, some would argue that Duckworth's populations used for her research, West Point cadets and National Spelling Bee contestants, are in fact, from privileged populations. As educators, implementing any curriculum or using a term like *grit* throughout the school needs to be done with care. We need to consider each student as an individual and provide for them what they need.

Duckworth and her colleagues designed a scale to measure grit. "Half of the questions are about responding resiliently to situations of failure and adversity or being a hard worker. The other half of the questionnaire is about having consistent interests-focused passions—over a long time" (Perkins-Gough, 2013). These items all speak to how Duckworth defines *grit*, which includes the components of passion, resilience, perseverance, and determination.

This refers, at times, to some of our most gifted or talented academic and athletic students. They may be gifted and/or talented, but they may not know how to fail. They struggle with failure. Furthermore, as Duckworth's research revealed, being gifted and/or talented, whether it be academically or through athletics, is no guarantee that these students are hardworking or passionate about something. See sidebar 9.2 for a link to try the "Grit Test."

Interestingly, Angela Duckworth and Carol Dweck have collaborated on a few projects and found that children who have more of a growth mindset tend to be grittier (Perkins-Gough, 2013). With that said, the connections between the elements of a growth mindset and grit are undeniable. For us to teach children to possess grit (if they don't already have it), using the elements of a growth mindset is the road map to get there. Teaching the value of practice and hard work will support most students as they develop a growth mindset and grit.

To learn more about Angela Duckworth and her work, see Sidebar 9.3.

> **Sidebar 9.3**
>
> For more information about Angela Duckworth and her work on grit, visit her website (https://angeladuckworth.com) and view her TED talk (https://youtu.be/H14bBuluwB8).

STRATEGIES TO BUILD AND DEVELOP RESILIENCY, A GROWTH MINDSET, AND GRIT

The following strategies can be used to support a child as they continue to develop and refine resiliency, a growth mindset, and grit.

- Again, use picture books! Don't forget, as mentioned earlier, picture books should be used at all levels to encourage developing resiliency, a growth mindset, and grit. Examining characters' decisions and the results of those decisions provides opportunities for students to see the outcomes of decision making. See sidebar 9.4 for a few books that can be used for this purpose.
- Similarly, as with picture books, writing is another strategy that can be used with all students. Studies show that writing about stressful experiences not only helps people to get better but also helps them from getting worse as they develop decision-making processes (Nakazawa, 2015). Short-term, focused writing in a classroom can have a beneficial effect. Writing about emotional concerns can help grades increase. Using focused prompts and connecting them to class readings can support children during the learning process.
- Working with community leaders of organizations in your local area to have your class contribute in some meaningful way to support others will help children to learn soft skills of compassion and gratitude. Pairing with a local soup kitchen, homeless shelter, or domestic violence agency for a project, the class can participate together, which will also build community within the classroom.
- Using media, whether it is inspirational movie clips or songs showing resiliency, growth mindset, and/or determination is an excellent approach to use during morning meeting or at the start of a class. This provides motivation for both younger and older students as they dissect lyrics or discuss movie scenes. These are two powerful ways to develop a positive mindset or foster a growth mindset.
- To further develop self-efficacy and stabilize physiological and affective arousal, relaxation practices can be used in the classroom (Everly & Firestone, 2013). Teaching these types of life skills and emotional regulation will lead to resiliency that will support children into adulthood. There are various breathing techniques that can be taught to children to help reduce anxiety, build resiliency, and focus on a growth mindset. Sidebar 9.5 is one example of a breathing exercise, titled "Hot Chocolate Breathing." There are also various applications that can be used in the classroom. One example is the Calm App. Sometimes these are free for educators to use or cost a nominal fee.

Sidebar 9.4. Books to Teach Grit and Resilience

1. *Oh, the Places You'll Go!* By Dr. Seuss (1990): Understanding that failure is inevitable and a key to building success. Rhymes and illustrations will lead the reader to learn how to respond to failures.
2. *The Hugging Tree: A Story About Resilience*, by Jill Neimark (2015): *The Hugging Tree* teaches children about hope and resilience. Rather than a just being lonely tree on a lonely cliff, the tree represents community and a place where people can get in touch with inner hopes and dreams.
3. *A Chair for My Mother*, by Vera B. Williams (2007): This Caldecott Honor Book exemplifies resilience after a family loses their belongings in a fire, as they try to save spare change to buy a new chair for Grandma.
4. *Sheila Rae, the Brave*, by Kevin Henkes (1996): Sheila Rae isn't afraid of anything, but when she gets lost, her little sister stands beside her and with her own bravery gets them both home.
5. *Ricky, the Rock That Couldn't Roll*, by Jay Miletsky (2018): From little pebbles to big boulders, the rocks get together to play and roll around their favorite hill, but Ricky, one of their friends, can't roll with them. All the other rocks are round, but Ricky is flat on one side. The rocks are determined to not leave their friend behind, so they set out to help Ricky roll around. This picture book highlights perseverance and triumph in the face of adversity, as well as the power of true friendship.
6. *The Most Magnificent Thing*, by Ashley Spires (2014): A young girl tries to create the "most magnificent thing," but when things don't go as planned, she becomes angry. Her dog encourages her to take a walk, and she comes back to the project and forges ahead. This book provides a perfect example of the reward of perseverance and creativity.
7. *After the Fall (How Humpty Dumpty Got Up Again)*, by Dan Santat (2017): This picture book reminds readers of all ages that life begins when you get back up.
8. *What Do You Do With a Chance?* by Kobi Yamada and Mae Besom (2018): A captivating story about a child who isn't sure what to make of a chance encounter and then discovers that when you have courage, take chances, and say yes to new experiences, amazing things can happen.
9. *The Book of Mistakes*, by Corinne Luyken (2017): A book about the creative process and the way "mistakes" can blossom into inspiration.
10. *My Mouth Is a Volcano*, by Julia Cook and Carrie Hartman (2006): Told from the perspective of Louis, the main character, this story provides parents, teachers, and counselors with an entertaining way to teach children the value of respecting others by listening and waiting for your turn to speak.

> **Sidebar 9.5. Hot Chocolate Breathing**
>
> Hot chocolate breathing is one example of an exercise that students can practice to bring calmness and center their body.
>
> 1. Pretend you are holding a cup of hot chocolate in both of your hands.
> 2. Bring the cup up close to your nose.
> 3. Breathe in the hot chocolate through your nose.
> 4. Imagine smelling the yummy hot chocolate. You can even close your eyes!
> 5. Slowly, exhale through your mouth as you pretend to blow the hot chocolate to cool it down.

- All children value mentors who support them, but children of trauma benefit from mentors to provide inspiration and optimism (Everly & Firestone, 2013). Mentors can be within the school, like other educators, staff members, or even parents. Mentors can also come from outside the classroom and in the local community. Reflecting with children about mentors and, as an educator, opening opportunities for parents, professionals, and community members to come into your classroom to deliver optimism as a mentor or role model would be a great way to foster resilience.
- Another strategy that can be implemented is "SIFTing Through the Mind," developed by Daniel Siegel (2012). This strategy is an extension of Daniel Siegel's (2012; 2018) work regarding a tool he has named "Wheel of Awareness." He uses the metaphor of a bicycle wheel to create a tool that can be used to create more well-being in a person's life. In the "SIFTing Through the Mind" strategy, as a new unit of study or lesson begins, children conduct "brain scans." The children close their eyes, and they notice what they are *s*ensing in their bodies when a topic is discussed, observing the *i*mages that are in their minds, the *f*eelings that are stirred, and the *t*houghts that take place in their minds (Siegel, 2012).
- Use choice boards as a way for students to choose from a list of choices for assignments. Providing choices gives children power and self-determination. Also, regardless of the outcome, they are responsible for their choice, and they have to understand consequences that may come from their choices.
- Developing mini-goals to long-term projects will support a growth mindset and build resiliency. Focusing on the process as they attain their goal is also an important piece of the process.
- As Carl Dweck (2006) mentioned, incorporating growth mindset language is a must. One example is the word *yet*. Instead of "I can't spell my words correctly," we need to encourage students to say, "I can't spell my words

Sidebar 9.6. Professional Development Books for Educators

The following list contains books to support educators as they learn more about grit, a growth mindset, and resiliency.

1. *Promoting Resilience in the Classroom: A Guide to Developing Emotional and Cognitive Skills*, by Carmel Cefai (2008): This book provides a framework to promote engagement and social-emotional competence in classrooms and throughout the school system.
2. *The Trauma Sensitive Classroom: Building Resilience With Compassionate Teaching*, by Patricia Jennings (2019): Jennings describes the effects trauma can have on the brain and mind, provides trauma-sensitive practices, and lastly, discusses how to build resilience and seek compassion for all learners.
3. *Mindset: The New Psychology of Success: How We Can Learn to Fulfill Our Potential*, by Carol Dweck (2006): In this seminal text, Dweck discusses the difference between a fixed and growth mindset and how to cultivate a growth mindset to motivate our kids and ourselves to reach our goals.
4. *Resilience at Work*, by Salvatore R. Maddi and Deboarah M. Khoshaba (2005): Maddi and Khoshaba explore resilience and the ways employees can possess a positive attitude to move toward transformational coping and overall resilience in the workplace.
5. *The Resiliency Advantage*, by Al Siebert (2005): This book is a "how to" book to help people become better at handling challenges and setbacks.
6. *Building Resilience in Children and Teens*, by Kenneth Girsburg and Martha Jablow (2015): In the latest edition of *Building Resilience in Children and Teens*, terms such as *stress*, *resilience*, and *grit* are reviewed. The importance of connection, character, and contribution is also discussed, as well as recommendations for increasing kids' sense of control and independence so that they can thrive throughout their lifetime.
7. *Grit: The Power of Passion and Perseverance*, by Angela Duckworth (2016): Angela Duckworth reveals how possessing passion, persistence, and perseverance can lead to having what she calls "grit."
8. *David and Goliath: Underdogs, Misfits and the Art of Battling Giants*, by Malcolm Gladwell (2013): Gladwell examines how people perceive challenges and urges the reader to rethink how we respond to life's obstacles.
9. *How Children Succeed: Grit, Curiosity and the Hidden Power of Character*, by Paul Tough (2013): Paul Tough uses brain research and his own firsthand accounts to make an argument that the qualities that matter most have to do with character; he also explains how schools can foster these traits in all children.
10. *The Gift of Failure*, by Jessica Lahey (2016): This is a great book for parents and teachers. Lahey emphasizes the importance of parents allowing children to experience disappointment and failure so that they can become resilient, successful adults.

correctly *yet*." We should be reinforcing that some things take time, effort, practice, and persistence to help our students to develop a growth mindset.
- Lastly, continue to learn and uncover the professional development opportunities that help and support you in the classroom to instill grit, resiliency, and a growth mindset within your own students. Sidebar 9.6 provides a list of professional development books you can read in your (very little, I'm sure) free time.

REFERENCES

American Psychological Association. (2014). *The road to resilience.* Author. http://www.apa.org/helpcenter/road-resilience.aspx

Bandura, A. (1997). *Self-efficacy: The exercise of control.* Freeman.

Cefai, C. (2008). *Promoting resilience in the classroom: A guide to developing pupils' emotional and cognitive skills.* Jessica Kingsley Publishers.

Condly, S. J. (2006). Resilience in children: A review of literature with implications for education. *Urban Education, 41*(3), 211–236. doi: 10.1177/0042085906287902

Craig, S. (2016). *Trauma-sensitive schools: Learning communities transforming children's lives, K–5.* Teachers College Press.

Duckworth, A. (2016). *Grit: The power of passion and perseverance.* Simon and Schuster.

Dweck, C. S. (2006). *Mindset: The new psychology of success.* Ballantine Books.

Dweck, C. S. (2015). Carol Dweck revisits the "growth mindset." *Education Week.* https://www.edweek.org/ew/articles/2015/09/23/carol-dweck-revisits-the-growth-mindset.html

Everly, G. S., & Firestone, R. M. (2013). Lessons for developing resilience. In E. Rossen & R. Hull (Eds.), *Supporting and education traumatized students: A guide for school-based professionals.* Oxford University Press.

Ginsburg, K. (2015). *Raising kids to thrive: Balancing love with expectations and protection with trust.* American Academy of Pediatrics.

Ginsburg , K. R., & Jablow, M. M. (2015). *Building resilience in children and teens: Giving kids roots and wings* (3rd ed.). American Academy of Pediatrics.

Jenkins, J. K. (2016). *The relationship between resilience, attachment, and emotional coping styles* [Unpublished doctoral dissertation]. Old Dominion University.

Jennings, P. A. (2019). *The trauma sensitive classroom: Building resilience with compassionate teaching.* W.W. Norton and Company.

Kaminsky, M., McCabe, O. L., Langlieb, A. M. & Everly, G. S. (2007). An evidence-informed model of human resistance, resilience, and recovery: The Johns Hopkins' outcome-derived paradigm for disaster mental health services. *Brief Treatment and Crisis Intervention, 7*(1), 1–11.

Konnikova, M. (2016). How people learn to become resilient. *The New Yorker.* https://www.newyorker.com/science/maria-konnikova/the-secret-formula-for-resilience

Nakazawa, D. J. (2015). *Childhood disrupted: How your biography becomes your biology, and how you can heal.* Atria Publishing.

Perkins-Gough, D. (2013). The significance of grit: A conversation with Angel Lee Duckworth. *Educational Leadership, 71*(1), 14–20.

Pietrzak R. H., & Southwick S. M. (2011). Psychological resilience in OEF-OIF veterans: Application of a novel classification approach and examination of demographic and psychosocial correlates. *Journal of Affect Disorders, 133*(3), 560–568.

Siegel, D. J. (2012). *The developing mind: How relationships and the brain interact to shape who we are* (2nd edition). Guilford Press.

Siegel, D. J. (2018). *Aware: The science and practice of presence—the groundbreaking meditation practice.* Random House.

Southwick, S. M., Bonanno, G. A., Masten, A. S., Panter-Brick, C., & Yehuda, R. (2014). Resilience definitions, theory, and challenges: interdisciplinary perspectives. *European Journal of Psychotraumatology, 5,* 10.3402/ejpt.v5.25338. http://doi.org/10.3402/ejpt.v5.25338

Williams, J. (n.d.). *What is grit, why kids need it, and how you can foster it.* https://afineparent.com/building-character/what-is-grit.html

10

Practicing Self-Care for Educators

> This chapter will provide:
> - an analysis of the terms *secondary traumatic stress, compassion fatigue,* and *vicarious trauma* and how they relate to teacher turnover;
> - information and frameworks to promote teacher resilience; and
> - a definition of *self-care* as well as tips, strategies, and activities for educators to better promote self-care to support themselves.

"Put your oxygen mask on first before placing oxygen masks on others." We've heard this stated many times on airplanes, and it's become a mantra for anyone in the caring profession. So, as educators in a caring profession, what does this truly mean? Sure, we will try our best to take care of ourselves, but *how* do we do that?

As we learned from the ACE study and current research, we now know that high rates of trauma (such as abuse, violence, natural disasters, and other adverse events) are experienced by school-aged children. Because of the high prevalence rates, it is more important now more than ever that we prepare educators to be trauma informed. We also need to ensure that as educators we are taking care of ourselves. Self-care is extremely important for us to build resilience and to support educators to discourage teacher attrition and turnover.

This chapter defines and discusses the three common terms associated with trauma: *compassion fatigue, vicarious trauma,* and *secondary traumatic stress.* The connection between secondary traumatic stress and teacher turnover will be analyzed. Also, we will give tips for promoting teacher resiliency and for self-care strategies that can be employed. Lastly, we will provide a list of resources for more information regarding self-care strategies. As a result of reading this chapter, you will hopefully understand the importance of placing your oxygen mask on first so that you can continue to serve the children you teach.

WHAT ARE SECONDARY TRAUMATIC STRESS, COMPASSION FATIGUE, AND VICARIOUS TRAUMA?

The National Child Traumatic Stress Network (2011) defines *secondary traumatic stress* as "the emotional duress that results when an individual hears about firsthand trauma experiences of another" (p. 2). Many of the symptoms a person who is facing secondary traumatic stress may experience mirror those of post-traumatic stress disorder (PTSD). They may experience variations in memory, worry about their own safety, have difficulty trusting others, and experience changes in their sense of control over their own activities and abilities. More symptoms of secondary traumatic stress are listed in sidebar 10.1.

Figley (1995) proposes the term *compassion fatigue*, which has been used interchangeably with *secondary traumatic stress*. Compassion fatigue occurs when "professionals feel there is nothing more they can do to help the

---

Sidebar 10.1. Symptoms and Conditions Associated With Secondary Traumatic Stress

- increased irritability
- guilt
- anger
- anxiety, which can result in sleeplessness
- fear
- hypervigilance
- hopelessness
- exhaustion
- inability to listen
- isolation

If you begin to notice a change in your behavior or that of a colleague and they are displaying some of these symptoms above, it's important to seek help or approach them to ask some questions. Instead of asking, "What's wrong with you?" a better question would be, "What happened to you?" A multidimensional approach for intervention and prevention will provide positive outcomes for all staff and faculty within the organization (adapted from National Child Traumatic Stress Network, 2011).

> **Sidebar 10.2. Possible Negative Reactions or Symptoms of Vicarious Trauma**
>
> The following is a list of possible symptoms or effects of someone who may be experiencing vicarious trauma. There may be similar symptoms as those noted with compassion fatigue, but overall vicarious trauma symptoms are more of a shift in a person's worldview.
>
> - emotionally numb or shutting down
> - easily distracted
> - feeling hopeless
> - feeling vulnerable or worrying excessively about dangerous situations
> - destructive coping or addictive behaviors
> - low motivation
> - lack of flexibility at a job

children they are responsible for no matter how much effort they expend" (Craig, 2016, p. 90).

Vicarious trauma is slightly different; it's the inner experience of the therapist or educator that is changed (National Child Traumatic Stress Network, 2011). When a person is engaged in an empathetic fashion with someone who has experienced trauma, the person may then have cognitive changes that occur as a result of hearing the other person's traumatic experiences. Focus is less on the theoretical term and more on the concealed cognitive changes a person may experience. As the National Child Traumatic Stress Network (2011) notes, it is the symptoms of vicarious trauma in the professional's cognitive frame of reference in the areas of trust, safety, control, esteem, and intimacy. Vicarious trauma can be experienced by people working in various fields such as victim services, law enforcement, counseling, fire services, and education. Overall, a person experiencing vicarious trauma will have a profound shift in their fundamental beliefs about the world.

For symptoms related to vicarious trauma, see sidebar 10.2.

Teacher Turnover

Professionals working with traumatized children are at risk for secondary traumatic stress, but research seems to indicate that the risk appears to be greater for women and individuals who tend to be more empathetic or who may have unresolved trauma (National Child Traumatic Stress Network, 2011). Furthermore, recent research also indicates that 46% of teachers say they feel high daily stress (Turner, 2016).

Between 19% and 30% of teachers times leave the profession within the first 5 years because of stress and other factors (Turner, 2016; Gibbs & Miller, 2014; Mansfield et al., 2016; Raab, 2018). Some of the issues educators have provided for leaving include high-stakes testing, lack of respect for the profession, physical conditions, student discipline, and motivational problems (Turner, 2016; Gibbs & Miller, 2014; Mulvahill, 2019). Stress and poor management of stressors has also been rated as one of the top reasons teachers leave the profession (Mulvahill, 2019; Carver-Thomas & Darling-Hammond, 2017).

Susan Craig (2016) makes a very good point when she states that many times teachers leave because they are unable to deliver instruction because of the interference of behaviors in the classroom. Many times, these behaviors are not solvable by what is taught in teacher-preparation programs, with such interventions as consequences, punishment, and contingency reinforcement. These interventions do not necessarily work because some of the behaviors may be correlated with early trauma and adverse experiences. They leave the field because they have exhausted their classroom-management techniques, and they themselves are exhausted.

Therefore, as stated previously, it is imperative that we ensure all teachers are trauma informed and they are provided with the pedagogical strategies necessary to support this vulnerable and diverse population. It is our purpose and duty as educators to assess and meet every single child where they are and then ensure each one thrives academically, socially, and emotionally (Aguilar, 2018).

Promoting Teacher Resilience

In chapter 9 we discussed strategies for building resilience within our students. Now, we will review how to promote teacher resilience. Aguilar (2018) notes that we can do a lot to boost our own individual resilience. Schools as systemic support systems can help educators cultivate resilience as well. As Craig (2016) notes, trauma sensitive schools "support teacher resilience by increasing access to known protections against stress, minimizing risk factors, and preparing them to use their relationship with children in positive manners" (p. 94).

As we think about ways to frame resiliency and how we can improve the resiliency of educators, there are a few frameworks we can use to support our efforts. Aguilar (2018) believes there needs to be three conversations concurrently to nurture resilience and change our schools. Interestingly, the suggestions Aguilar provides are parallel to Bronfenbrenner's ecological systems theory of child development, which we discussed in chapter 3. Aguilar (2018) first believes we need to foster and improve our own well-being. Self-care strategies are an excellent way to support this first step. Later we will explore self-care strategies that will support us as educators as we cultivate resiliency.

Craig (2016) would agree with this thinking since she notes the importance of using coping strategies and self-regulation to boost the promotion of teacher resilience. Problem-solving skills, remaining objective, and employing coping mechanisms when instructional goals are difficult to reach, when giving a student negative feedback, or when a student struggles with the material, can be a regular occurrence in the classroom. Teachers should be prepared to employ coping strategies during these situations.

Self-regulation is another component needed for teacher resilience (Craig, 2016). Educators and administrators alike need to be prepared to deescalate student behaviors. Strategies and internal support systems are needed, as they respond to the behaviors of the student attentively.

Once we pay attention to our own resilience, this will afford us the opportunity to transform our schools and tackle other systemic conditions. The second conversation that needs to occur includes the opportunity for us to review our organizational conditions. This includes the strength of our leaders in our school and reviewing our basic operational routines and systems.

Furthermore, Aguilar (2018) discusses the importance of school culture, as was covered and discussed earlier in chapter 8. The organizational conditions should be optimal so that all educators, even those possessing a high level of resilience, are willing to stay in the current working environment.

Lastly, systemic conditions should be reviewed. (Think of the macrosystem from Bronfenbrenner's theory.) These include the political and economic contexts of our education system (Aguilar, 2018) as well as the racism, classism, and sexism that exist in our schools. Teacher-preparation programs need to improve, and to that point, many would argue that teachers should be paid fairly for all that they do. The entire structure of our U.S. education system should be examined with educators working alongside policymakers to effectively create change.

Another piece of resiliency includes acquiring coping and self-care strategies to ensure all educators are able to support traumatized children in the classroom. In the next section, we will define *self-care* and then provide tips that can be used for self-care for all educators.

DEFINING *SELF-CARE* FOR EDUCATORS

Self-care—we've heard the term, but what does it mean, and how do we do it within our busy lifestyles? At times there are many reasons we do not initiate self-care. We think we are too busy to take care of ourselves. We have a hard time saying "no" to people we care about. We put off self-care because we feel we have more urgent matters at hand. Self-care is not selfish, and it is really important that as educators we make the time to add it to our daily routines.

Boogren (2018) believes in daily self-care and has noted Cook-Cottone's (2015) definition of *self-care*: "daily process of being aware of and attending to one's basic physiological and emotional needs including the shaping of one's daily routine, relationships, and environment" (p. 297). The World Health Organization (2009) views self-care from a broader stance encompassing families and communities, stating, "Self-care is the ability of individuals, families and communities to promote health, prevent disease, and maintain health and to cope with illness and disability with or without the support of a health-care provider."

People who are resilient are committed to taking care of themselves. We all strive for daily self-care, and if you are not there yet, try to make that an ultimate goal—to take a few moments for yourself each day. And the good news is self-care can happen at any time, and in any moment. It's about self-compassion and not driven by an effort to become more or better. It's meeting yourself where you are at that moment.

With that said, I will still provide some strategies you may want to try to add to your self-care repertoire with the caveat that you remember you don't have to "do" something to initiate self-care. Being alone with your thoughts, quietly for a few moments a day, could be self-care.

There are a few frameworks that could be used to implement a self-care plan. One framework Boogren (2018) notes uses Abraham Maslow's Hierarchy of Needs. Maslow's (1943; 1954) theory resonates when we consider a trauma-informed approach regardless if it is employed for the person directly affected by trauma or for a person experiencing secondary trauma.

In Maslow's theory, our needs progress through levels. We need to feel secure at each level or need before we can consider reaching self-actualization, which is our motivation to reach our full potential. The first four levels need to be met to avoid negative physical or psychological sensations (Boogren, 2018).

The first level is physiological needs, which includes food, water, sleep, and shelter. The next level is our safety or security needs, such as body, financial or employment, and safety of our family. The third level is our love and belonging needs and includes our friendships, intimacy, and family relationships. The last level, self-actualization, includes problem solving, creativity, and acceptance of facts.

By using this model, we can check in with ourselves to consider if we have met our needs, and if not, we can do a quick self-care pick-up. One example of when our needs are not met is the slang term *hangry*. When a person is hungry and glucose or blood sugar drops, they may become angry, and the term *hangry* can be used to describe this physiological feeling.

TIPS FOR SELF-CARE

This model may be helpful as we are mindful of our needs. There are other steps that we can use to make time for self-care. The following three steps Gonzalez (2017) notes are essential for all educators or anyone in the helping profession to use as they take care of themselves.

1. Build in rest. Instead of working to the point of exhaustion, we need to view rest as a crucial tool for productivity. Being intentional and adding in rest, like being silent and still for a few moments a day, can benefit productivity.
2. Streamline your schedule, and simplify your work life. Evaluate priorities, and shift tasks for items that are not necessary at the moment. Using available resources that can be found online or resources your colleagues may have to support your needs in the classroom can help you to work smarter and not harder. Also, learning how to say "no" to tasks or items you do not have time for will help to streamline your schedule.
3. Pair a new self-care habit with a consistent routine. Combining a new self-care item like deep breathing for 60 seconds at the end of a school day or after lunch every day will help to ensure the self-care strategy becomes a new habit.

Self-care will look different for each person. We should have a repertoire of strategies and activities so that we can vary or use the strategies that are most appealing to our lifestyle and personalities. It's extremely important that you also have a cadre of friends, family, and colleagues that you can rely on to support you when you feel you need it. Building and cultivating a strong peer network in the school environment to support each other can help lessen work-related stress. Support networks can be a positive resource.

The following is a list of self-care strategies you can implement to support yourself and ensure you are "wearing your oxygen mask first." Of course, none of these should take the place of professional medical attention, and if you feel you need medical attention, it is important that you obtain it. Before instituting any type of self-care, you may want to consider completing a self-care checklist, such as those listed in sidebar 10.3.

> **Sidebar 10.3. Self-Care Checklists and Self-Tests**
>
> Before implementing new self-care strategies or forming healthy new habits, completing self-tests can help determine compassion fatigue and life stress level. These are not to be used to replace qualified medical care but could help to determine if further assistance is needed.
>
> 1. http://www.compassionfatigue.org/pages/selftest.html: This website provides an explanation and lists signs of compassion fatigue. Three self-tests are also provided: the Professional Quality of Life Self-Test, Life Stress Self-Test, and Empathy Test.
> 2. Boogren (2018) provides a self-care survey in her book; it can also be found by creating a free account at go.SolutionTree.com/instruction.

- Use a calendar to note the self-care you will provide yourself each day. See figure 10.1 for self-care activities that can be introduced each month.
- Keep a gratitude journal. Using a gratitude journal daily can have many benefits like reducing stress levels, keeping negative emotions at bay, improving your health, and improving sleep.
- Read. As we discussed in chapter 7, there are many benefits of bibliotherapy, and many positive effects reading can have on someone who is struggling. Reading is therapeutic and can be part of a self-care regimen.
- Walking, biking, yoga, or any form of exercise is necessary for our overall health and self-care.
- Use mindfulness, meditation, and prayer. Mindfulness has been proven to benefit young people as well and is something that can be taught in the classroom throughout the day to keep students centered.
- Sleep: making time for a healthy number of hours of sleep each night can regulate our emotional state.
- Essential oils can reduce stress and anxiety and induce a tranquil feeling. Depending on the essential oil, some can boost cognitive function, mood, and memory.
- Self-care can include making time on a regular basis for a hobby or activity you enjoy, such as reading, knitting, exercising, gardening, crafting, or cooking.
- A lot of the items listed have been relatively inexpensive or free. Self-care activities like regular haircuts, manicures, pedicures, face masks, or massages can rejuvenate us as well.
- Many years ago, I began a "smile file." These including notes from students, parents, and colleagues that affected me in a positive manner. Pulling out notes from past students, parents, or colleagues helps to remind me of the influence I have had on my students and in the field of education.

Figure 10.1 Monthly self-care activities for teachers. *Source:* Brooke Khan

- Using stress balls throughout the day can help relieve stress.

As educators, we need to be resilient, be determined, and have grit ourselves. Cultivating our own resilience will enable us to build resilience, grit, and determination in our students. All of our students, especially our most vulnerable students such as children of trauma, deserve the best of us.

We learned about adverse childhood experience, including specifically domestic violence. We learned the impact that trauma can have on children's development, language, memory, and the acquiring of reading and writing skills. We learned ways to use children's literature to benefit all children positively in the classroom. We learned the importance of relationships, self-regulation, and a positive school climate. We need to continue to implement what we've learned and remain committed to educating ourselves as we use best practices and employ the best pedagogical tools in our schools and classrooms. We can do this, and we will make a difference in the lives of all of the students we teach on a daily basis. After all, in the words of esteemed educator Rita Pierson (2013) in her fabulous TED Talk, "We're educators. We're born to make a difference."

REFERENCES

Aguilar, E. (2018). *Onward: Cultivating emotional resilience in educators*. Jossey-Bass.

Boogren, T. H. (2018). *Take time for you: Self-care action plans for educators*. Solution Tree Press.

Carver-Thomas, D., & Darling-Hammond, L. (2017). *Teacher turnover: Why it matters and what we can do about it* [Policy brief]. Learning Policy Institute. https://learningpolicyinstitute.org/sites/default/files/product-files/Teacher_Turnover_BRIEF.pdf

Cook-Cottone, C. P. (2015). *Mindfulness and yoga for self-regulation: A primer for mental health professionals*. Springer.

Craig, S. (2016). *Trauma-sensitive schools: Learning communities transforming children's lives, K–5*. Teachers College Press.

Figley, C. R. (1995). Compassion fatigue as secondary traumatic stress disorder: An overview. In C. R. Figley (Ed.), *Compassion fatigue: Coping with secondary traumatic stress disorder in those who treat the traumatized* (pp. 1–20). Brunner/Mazel.

Gibbs, S., & Miller, A. (2014). Teachers' resilience and well-being: A role for educational psychology. *Teachers and Teaching: Theory and Practice, 20*, 609–621.

Gonzalez, J. (2017). *Why it's so hard for teachers to take care of themselves (and 4 ways to start)*. https://www.cultofpedagogy.com/teacher-self-care.

Mansfield, C. F., Beltman, S., Broadley, T., & Weatherby-Fell, N. (2016). Building resilience in teacher education: An evidenced informed framework. *Teaching and Teacher Education, 54,* 77–87.

Maslow, A. H. (1943). A theory of human motivation. *Psychological Review, 50*(4), 370–396.

Maslow, A. H. (1954). *Motivation and personality.* Harper.

Mulvahill, E. (2019, June 14). *Why teachers quit.* We Are Teachers. https://www.weareteachers.com/why-teachers-quit

National Child Traumatic Stress Network. (2011). *Secondary traumatic stress: A fact sheet for child-serving professionals* [Pamphlet]. https://www.nctsn.org/resources/secondary-traumatic-stress-fact-sheet-child-serving-professionals

Pierson, R. (2013). Every kid needs a champion. *TED Talks Education.* https://www.ted.com/talks/rita_pierson_every_kid_needs_a_champion?utm_campaign=social&utm_medium=referral&utm_source=t.co&utm_content=talk&utm_term=education

Raab, R. R. (2018). A statistic's five years: A story of teacher attrition. *Qualitative Inquiry, 24*(8), 583–591.

Turner, C. (2016). Teachers are stressed, and that should stress us all. *NPR.* https://www.npr.org/sections/ed/2016/12/30/505432203/teachers-are-stressed-and-that-should-stress-us-all

World Health Organization. (2009). *Self-care in the context of primary health care.* Report of the Regional Consultation Bangkok, Thailand. https://isfglobal.org/what-is-self-care

About the Author

Colleen Lelli, Ed.D., is an associate professor in the Educational Specialists Department and the director of the Center for Children of Trauma and Domestic Violence Education at Cabrini University in Pennsylvania. Dr. Lelli has over 27 years of experience in the education field. She began her career teaching preschool children and then taught students with various disabilities at the high school level in Pottsgrove, Pennsylvania.

Dr. Lelli, now in her 18th year in higher education as of this writing, has taught both undergraduate and graduate courses including reading methods courses, special education methods courses, domestic violence education courses, and autism methodology courses. Her research interests include: developing special education advocacy and support; enhancing preservice and in-service teachers' knowledge of domestic violence; and growing their abilities to support the learning of those who have witnessed trauma. One key focus is using children's literature to advocate for children with special needs (e.g., helping children of trauma gain resilience). Additionally, Dr. Lelli has published and presented while providing teachers and professionals key strategies to support children of trauma to learn effectively in the classroom. Her presentations and work have been recognized widely, nationally and internationally. In May of 2020, Dr. Lelli was awarded the prestigious Lindback Distinguished Teaching Award, which recognizes outstanding teaching for faculty at colleges and universities in Pennsylvania and New Jersey.

In her free time, Dr. Lelli serves as co-president of the board of directors for a local domestic violence agency and as a board member of a local agency representing sexual assault victims. She lives in Limerick, Pennsylvania, with her husband Michael, her son Michael, her daughter Julianna, and her favorite dog Reggie.

www.ingramcontent.com/pod-product-compliance
Lightning Source LLC
Chambersburg PA
CBHW021851300426
44115CB00005B/107